Learn Japanese for Adult Beginners

Speak Japanese In 30 Days!

3 Books in 1

Explore to Win

Table of Contents

BOOK 3

Japanese Grammar and Sentence Patterns for Beginners

$~~\sout{500}~~500+$ FREE BONUSES

Japanese Video Lessons

Japanese Flashcards + 30-Day Study Plan

Japanese Short Stories Audiobook

Japanese Conversation Dialogues

Japanese Email Crash Course

Premium Japanese Learning Software

Scan QR code to claim your bonuses

— OR —

visit bit.ly/3shFlJg

BOOK 1

Learn Japanese for Adult Beginners:

Master Basic Hiragana, Katakana, and Kanji in 30 Days!

Explore to Win

Book Description

Are you a complete beginner eager to learn Japanese from scratch? Do you want to master the basics of Japanese grammar, vocabulary, and the complex writing systems? Are you looking for a step-by-step guide that makes learning Japanese straightforward and effective?

If you answered yes to any of these questions, then this book is for you!

"Learn Japanese for Adult Beginners: Master Basic Hiragana, Katakana, and Kanji in 30 Days!" is designed to provide new learners with the foundational tools to start reading, writing, and speaking Japanese confidently in just one month. This comprehensive guide breaks down the essentials of the Japanese language with clear explanations, structured lessons, and interactive exercises, making your learning journey both enjoyable and rewarding.

Inside this guide, you'll find:

- **Simple, step-by-step lessons** covering everything from the basics of Hiragana and Katakana to understanding essential Kanji characters, ensuring a smooth and structured learning experience
- **Detailed stroke-by-stroke instructions** to help you master the writing of each script, with visual guides to reinforce your learning
- **Pronunciation and speaking tips** to ensure you sound natural when speaking Japanese, even if you've never studied a language with different sounds before
- **Exercises at the end of each chapter** to strengthen your understanding and build confidence in using what you've learned
- **Real-world examples and dialogues**, allowing you to practice reading and comprehension with practical scenarios

You'll also benefit from:

- A **structured approach** to mastering the three main scripts—Hiragana, Katakana, and Kanji— breaking down what might seem overwhelming into manageable lessons
- **Key takeaways** and practice exercises that ensure you can apply what you've learned right away in real-life conversations
- **Cultural insights** to deepen your understanding of the language and its unique context, making your learning experience richer and more meaningful

Imagine being able to read basic Japanese texts, understand simple conversations, and respond confidently—whether you're planning to visit Japan, exploring the language's cultural richness, or learning for personal growth.

Whether you're starting your Japanese journey or refreshing your foundational skills, **"Learn Japanese for Adult Beginners"** is your ultimate guide to success.

Ready to take your first step toward Japanese fluency? **Grab your copy today and start learning Japanese with confidence!**

Click "Add to Cart" and begin your journey to mastering Japanese in just 30 days!

Introduction

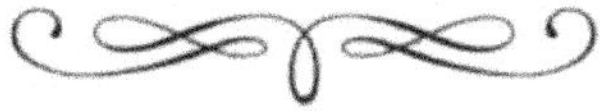

"To learn a language is to have one more window from which to look at the world."

– Chinese Proverb

Are you excited to learn Japanese but feel overwhelmed by the complex scripts, unfamiliar grammar structures, and new sounds? Does the thought of memorizing three different writing systems—Hiragana, Katakana, and Kanji—make you wonder where to begin? If so, you're not alone—but rest assured, you've found the right guide.

Learn Japanese for Adult Beginners is more than just a language manual; it's a structured learning journey designed to help you master the essentials of Japanese in just 30 days. Whether you're learning Japanese for travel, work, cultural appreciation, or simply personal growth, this book is crafted to build your confidence in reading, writing, and speaking Japanese.

Many learners find Japanese challenging, not because it's too difficult, but because they don't have the right approach or resources. The language has its own unique beauty, but starting with its three distinct scripts can seem daunting. Add in new vocabulary, sentence patterns, and pronunciation rules, and it's easy to feel lost. But here's the good news: learning Japanese can be easier and more rewarding than you think!

This book will guide you step-by-step through the core elements of Japanese, from understanding Hiragana, Katakana, and essential Kanji to constructing basic sentences and holding everyday conversations. You'll learn how to approach Japanese grammar in a straightforward, easy-to-understand manner, with interactive exercises that will reinforce your progress and help you gain confidence.

Each chapter will build on what you've learned, starting with the fundamentals of reading and writing Japanese scripts and progressing to key grammar rules, pronunciation tips, and useful phrases. You'll master essential expressions for daily conversations, whether you're introducing yourself, asking for directions, or ordering food. By the end of this book, you'll be able to hold basic conversations and read simple Japanese texts.

We understand that learning a new language as an adult comes with unique challenges. That's why this book is designed specifically for adult learners, offering clear explanations, practical exercises, and real-world examples that make learning Japanese engaging and accessible. You'll find that each new concept is presented in a way that's easy to grasp, and every chapter concludes with a set of exercises to solidify your understanding.

Our team has years of experience helping adult learners master new languages, and we've designed this book to be a reliable companion on your Japanese learning journey. With each chapter, you'll grow more confident in your ability to read and speak Japanese, understand its sentence structures, and apply your knowledge in everyday scenarios.

To ensure you retain the key concepts, we've included **Key Takeaways** at the end of each lesson, summarizing the most important points. You'll also find **practical exercises** throughout the book to practice new vocabulary, sentence patterns, and writing skills, making your learning both thorough and effective.

Learning Japanese is more than just memorizing characters and grammar—it's about connecting with a rich cultural heritage and understanding a language that has been shaped by centuries of tradition and innovation. Whether you're planning to use Japanese in personal or professional settings or simply want to appreciate its beauty, this book will give you the tools you need to communicate with confidence.

Now that you've taken the first step, it's time to dive in and embrace the process of learning Japanese. With the guidance, exercises, and practical tips in this book, you'll quickly build the skills you need to feel comfortable speaking and reading Japanese in everyday situations.

So, are you ready to begin your 30-day journey toward mastering Japanese? Let's start with the basics—learning the Japanese writing system and pronunciation rules—so you can start speaking Japanese from day one.

Let's begin your **Japanese language journey!**

Chapter 1: Overview of the Japanese Writing System

"Learning another language is not only learning different words for the same things, but learning another way to think about things."

– Flora Lewis

Welcome to the start of your Japanese language journey! Before diving into vocabulary, grammar, or conversations, it's crucial to understand the foundation of the language—the writing system. Japanese is unique in that it uses three distinct scripts: Hiragana, Katakana, and Kanji. These scripts are interwoven to create the rich tapestry of written Japanese, each serving a specific purpose and lending depth to the language.

For many new learners, the idea of mastering three separate scripts might seem intimidating. But here's the good news: once you understand how and when each script is used, you'll see that Japanese writing is more logical and organized than it first appears. In fact, the scripts complement one another, making reading and writing more precise and more nuanced.

This chapter will provide an overview of the Japanese writing system, explain the roles of Hiragana, Katakana, and Kanji, and show you when and how to use each script. By the end, you'll have a strong grasp of the foundational structure of the Japanese language, setting you up for success as you move forward.

Let's begin by understanding the **roles and characteristics of each script in detail.**

Understanding the Roles of Hiragana, Katakana, and Kanji

The Japanese writing system is composed of three different scripts, each serving its own purpose: **Hiragana**, **Katakana**, and **Kanji**. While these scripts might seem overwhelming at first, knowing the role of each one will help you see how they work together to form a cohesive system.

1. Hiragana: The Foundation Script

Hiragana is the most basic of the three scripts and is often the first one that Japanese learners study. It is primarily used for native Japanese words and grammatical functions. Think of Hiragana as the script that holds the language together.

- **Characteristics**:
  - Contains **46 basic characters** that represent distinct sounds
  - Curved and flowing strokes, making it visually softer than Katakana
  - Each character represents a syllable, combining a consonant and vowel (e.g., か = *ka*, す = *su*).

- - Used to spell out **grammatical particles**, verb endings, and native Japanese words that don't have a Kanji representation
- **Examples of Usage**:
  - **Particles** (function words that connect parts of a sentence): は (*wa*), を (*wo*)
  - **Verb and adjective endings**: 食べる (*taberu* - to eat), 大きい (*ookii* - big)
  - **Words for children** or beginners often appear solely in Hiragana: さくら (*sakura* - cherry blossom)
- **Why It's Important**:
  - Hiragana is crucial for reading and understanding Japanese grammar.
  - Learning Hiragana thoroughly will also help you read furigana (small Hiragana characters used to show the pronunciation of Kanji).

2. Katakana: The Script for Foreign Words and Emphasis

Katakana is used to write foreign words and names, loanwords, onomatopoeia, and for emphasis. It has a more angular and sharp appearance compared to Hiragana.

- **Characteristics**:
  - Contains the **same 46 sounds** as Hiragana but uses a different set of symbols
  - Visually sharper and more straightforward, with a rigid and angular design
  - Each character represents a syllable (e.g., カ = *ka*, ス = *su*)
- **Examples of Usage**:
  - **Foreign words and loanwords**: テレビ (*terebi* - television), コンピュータ (*konpyuta* - computer)
  - **Foreign names**: ジョン (*Jon* - John), アン (*An* - Ann)
  - **Onomatopoeia**: ワンワン (*wan wan* - the sound of a dog barking), ピカピカ (*pika pika* - something shiny)
  - **Emphasis**: Sometimes used for emphasis in advertising or to make certain words stand out in text.
- **Why It's Important**:
  - Understanding Katakana is essential for reading words borrowed from other languages and names of places or people.
  - Many foods, brands, and technical terms appear in Katakana.

3. Kanji: The Script of Symbols and Meanings

Kanji are complex characters borrowed from Chinese that carry meanings rather than just sounds. Each Kanji can have multiple readings and meanings, depending on its context.

- **Characteristics**:
  - There are **thousands of Kanji characters** used in Japanese, but **around 2,000 are commonly used** for daily life.
  - Each Kanji represents an idea or concept (e.g., 木 = *ki* - tree, 火 = *hi* - fire).
  - Kanji can stand alone or combine with other Kanji or Hiragana to form new words.
- **Readings**:
  - **On'yomi** (音読み - "sound reading"): Derived from the original Chinese pronunciation (e.g., 学 = *gaku* as in 学校 - *gakkou* - school)
  - **Kun'yomi** (訓読み - "meaning reading"): Native Japanese reading, often used when the Kanji is alone (e.g., 学 = *manabu* - to learn)
- **Examples of Usage**:
  - **Nouns**: 水 (*mizu* - water), 山 (*yama* - mountain).
  - **Verbs and Adjectives** (often combined with Hiragana endings): 飲む (*nomu* - to drink), 美しい (*utsukushii* - beautiful).
  - **Proper Names**: Common in family names and place names (e.g., 東京 - *Tokyo*).
- **Why It's Important**:
  - Kanji adds depth and clarity to Japanese sentences by reducing ambiguity.
  - It allows for quicker reading and understanding since Kanji carries meaning independently of context.

How These Scripts Work Together

In everyday Japanese text, all three scripts are used together seamlessly:

- **Hiragana** is used for grammatical purposes, such as particles and verb endings.
- **Katakana** is used for foreign loanwords or names.
- **Kanji** is used for the core meaning of words, particularly nouns, verbs, and adjectives.

Example Sentence Breakdown:

私はテレビを見ます。 (*Watashi wa terebi o mimasu.* - I watch television.)

- 私は (*watashi wa*) → "I" (Kanji + Hiragana)
- テレビ (*terebi*) → "Television" (Katakana)
- を (*wo*) → Grammatical particle (Hiragana)
- 見ます (*mimasu*) → "Watch" (Kanji + Hiragana)

This combination of scripts is one of the defining features of Japanese and is what makes learning the language both fascinating and rewarding.

When and How to Use Each Script

Now that you know the basic roles of **Hiragana**, **Katakana**, and **Kanji**, let's dive into when and how to use each script in everyday Japanese.

Understanding their specific applications will help you read and write more confidently, as each script has clear purposes in forming words, phrases, and sentences.

1. When to Use Hiragana

Hiragana is often the backbone of Japanese writing, providing the structure and grammatical framework for sentences. It is primarily used for:

- **Grammatical Functions**:
  - Hiragana is used to spell out **particles** (small grammatical markers that indicate the relationship between words) such as は (*wa* - topic marker), が (*ga* - subject marker), and を (*wo* - object marker).
  - It is also used to express **verb endings** and **adjective conjugations** (e.g., 食べます - *tabemasu* - to eat; 大きい - *ookii* - big).
- **Writing Native Japanese Words**:
  - Words that don't have a specific Kanji representation, such as ねこ (*neko* - cat) and かわいい (*kawaii* - cute), are written using Hiragana.
- **Reading Assistance for Kanji**:
  - **Furigana**: Small Hiragana characters are placed above or beside difficult Kanji to indicate pronunciation. This is common in children's books and for foreign learners.

Examples of When to Use Hiragana:

- **Particles**: これはペンです。 (*Kore wa pen desu.* - This is a pen.)
- **Native Words**: わたしはがっこうへいきます。 (*Watashi wa gakkou e ikimasu.* - I am going to school.)
- **Verb Conjugation**: 見ています。 (*Miteimasu.* - Watching.)

Key Points:

- Beginners should focus on mastering Hiragana first, as it forms the foundation of Japanese grammar.
- Use Hiragana for particles, verb and adjective endings, and native words not covered by Kanji.

2. When to Use Katakana

Katakana is primarily used to represent foreign words and technical terms, as well as for emphasis. It is often the script you'll see when reading loanwords or the names of imported products.

- **Foreign Loanwords**:
  - Words borrowed from other languages, such as English, are written in Katakana. This includes food items, technology terms, and names.
  - Examples:
    - バナナ (*banana* - banana)
    - コンピュータ (*konpyu-ta* - computer)
    - コーヒー (*ko-hi-* - coffee)
- **Foreign Names and Places**:
  - Foreign names and countries are written in Katakana.
  - Examples: ジョン (*Jon* - John), アメリカ (*Amerika* - America), フランス (*Furansu* - France)
- **Scientific and Technical Terms**:
  - Katakana is used for scientific terms, animal names, and some plant names.
  - Examples: ゴリラ (*gorira* - gorilla), バクテリア (*bakuteria* - bacteria)
- **Onomatopoeia and Emphasis**:
  - Katakana is often used to emphasize sounds or actions, especially in manga or advertisements.
  - Examples: ドキドキ (*dokidoki* - heartbeat), ピカピカ (*pikapika* - sparkle)

Key Points:

- Use Katakana for all **non-Japanese names**, **loanwords**, and **scientific terms**.
- Katakana is also used to make certain words stand out visually, similar to italics in English.

3. When to Use Kanji

Kanji is used for the **core meaning** of most nouns, verbs, adjectives, and adverbs. It allows Japanese to be written in a more compact and nuanced way. Each Kanji character carries a specific meaning, and many have multiple readings depending on context.

- **Nouns**: Most nouns are represented using Kanji.
  - Examples: 水 (*mizu* - water), 木 (*ki* - tree), 山 (*yama* - mountain)
- **Verbs and Adjectives**:
  - The **root** of most verbs and adjectives are written in Kanji, while the conjugated endings are in Hiragana.
  - Examples: 食べる (*taberu* - to eat), 飲む (*nomu* - to drink), 高い (*takai* - tall/high)
- **Proper Names**:
  - Kanji is used extensively in Japanese names and place names.

- ○ Examples: 山田 (*Yamada* - a common surname), 東京 (*Tokyo* - the capital city)
- **Compound Words**:
  - ○ Kanji is combined to form compound words with complex meanings.
  - ○ Example: 電話 (*denwa* - telephone, made up of 電 - electricity and 話 - talk)

Key Points:

- Use Kanji for most **nouns, verb roots, and adjectives**.
- If a word has a Kanji representation, using it will make your writing clearer and more formal.

Using the Scripts Together in a Sentence

In a typical Japanese sentence, all three scripts work together to form a coherent and structured text. Here's how they might appear together:

Sentence Example:
私はテレビを見ます。 (*Watashi wa terebi o mimasu.* - I watch television.)

- 私は → "I" (私 - Kanji for *watashi*; は - Hiragana particle *wa*)
- テレビ → "television" (Katakana for *terebi*)
- を → Particle marking the object (Hiragana *wo*)
- 見ます → "Watch" (見 - Kanji for the verb *miru*, meaning to watch; ます - Hiragana for verb ending *masu*)

This sentence illustrates how each script contributes to the meaning and structure of the language: Kanji for the core meaning, Hiragana for grammar and pronunciation, and Katakana for foreign terms.

Tips for Remembering When to Use Each Script

- **Hiragana**: Use for **native words, particles**, and **verb/adjective endings**.
- **Katakana**: Use for **foreign words, emphasis**, and **technical terms**.
- **Kanji**: Use for the **core meanings** of words—especially for nouns, verbs, and adjectives.

By understanding these rules, you'll be able to decipher Japanese sentences more easily and confidently.

Key Takeaways

- ❖ **Japanese uses three scripts**—Hiragana, Katakana, and Kanji—each with distinct roles and characteristics.

- ❖ **Hiragana** is used for grammatical purposes, verb endings, and native Japanese words.

- ❖ **Katakana** is used for foreign words, names, and emphasis.

- ❖ **Kanji** conveys core meanings and is used for most nouns, verbs, and adjectives.

- ❖ Learning when to use each script is essential for reading and writing in Japanese, as they often appear together in the same sentence.

Exercises

Exercise 1: Identify the Script
Label each word below as **Hiragana (H)**, **Katakana (K)**, or **Kanji (J)**:

1. はな (＿＿＿)
2. コンピュータ (＿＿＿)
3. 日本 (＿＿＿)
4. すし (＿＿＿)
5. テーブル (＿＿＿)
6. 山 (＿＿＿)
7. 先生 (＿＿＿)
8. あおい (＿＿＿)
9. サラダ (＿＿＿)
10. 東京 (＿＿＿)

Exercise 2: Fill in the Script
Write the following words using the correct script based on the rules provided:

1. **Tokyo** (City Name): ＿＿＿＿＿＿＿＿＿＿＿＿＿
2. **Apple** (Foreign Food Item): ＿＿＿＿＿＿＿＿＿＿＿＿
3. **Water** (Basic Noun): ＿＿＿＿＿＿＿＿＿＿＿＿
4. **To Eat** (Verb with Conjugation): ＿＿＿＿＿＿＿＿＿＿＿＿
5. **Library** (Compound Noun): ＿＿＿＿＿＿＿＿＿＿＿＿

Exercise 3: Mixed Script Sentence
Translate the following into a mixed-script Japanese sentence using Hiragana, Katakana, and Kanji appropriately:

1. **I drink coffee.**
2. **She reads books.**
3. **We eat sushi.**

Answer Key

Exercise 1: Identify the Script

1. はな (H)
2. コンピュータ (K)
3. 日本 (J)
4. すし (H)
5. テーブル (K)
6. 山 (J)
7. 先生 (J)
8. あおい (H)
9. サラダ (K)
10. 東京 (J)

Exercise 2: Fill in the Script

1. **Tokyo** (City Name): 東京
2. **Apple** (Foreign Food Item): リンゴ
3. **Water** (Basic Noun): 水
4. **To Eat** (Verb with Conjugation): 食べる
5. **Library** (Compound Noun): 図書館

Exercise 3: Mixed Script Sentence

1. **I drink coffee.** → 私はコーヒーを飲みます。 (*Watashi wa ko-hi- o nomimasu.*)
2. **She reads books.** → 彼女は本を読みます。 (*Kanojo wa hon o yomimasu.*)
3. **We eat sushi.** → 私たちはすしを食べます。 (*Watashitachi wa sushi o tabemasu.*)

Chapter 2: Mastering Hiragana from Scratch

"Small daily improvements over time lead to stunning results."
– Robin Sharma

Now that you understand the Japanese writing system, it's time to start building your foundation by mastering **Hiragana**. As the first script introduced to beginners, Hiragana forms the backbone of Japanese grammar and is essential for reading, writing, and pronunciation. By understanding Hiragana, you'll learn to read basic Japanese sentences, understand simple words, and begin constructing sentences on your own.

This chapter will guide you step-by-step through the **complete Hiragana character set**. You'll learn the correct **stroke order** for each character, practice writing them out, and understand how each character is pronounced. Mastering Hiragana is like setting the cornerstone of a building—you'll build upon this skill in all future learning.

With consistent practice and careful attention to stroke order, you'll find that writing Hiragana becomes second nature. By the end of this chapter, you'll be able to confidently read and write all **46 basic Hiragana characters** and recognize how they are used in simple Japanese words and phrases.

Let's get started by exploring the complete Hiragana character set!

The Complete Hiragana Character Set

Hiragana consists of **46 basic characters**, each representing a unique syllable. This set forms the core sounds of the Japanese language. Each character is composed of a combination of a **consonant** and a **vowel** (e.g., か = *ka*) or just a vowel sound (e.g., あ = *a*).

Understanding and mastering these characters is the first step in developing reading and writing fluency.

Hiragana Chart Overview

Below is a chart of the **basic Hiragana characters** divided by their corresponding vowels (a, i, u, e, o). Spend time getting familiar with each row and column to see how they relate to one another.

Vowels	A	I	U	E	O
K	か (*ka*)	き (*ki*)	く (*ku*)	け (*ke*)	こ (*ko*)
S	さ (*sa*)	し (*shi*)	す (*su*)	せ (*se*)	そ (*so*)

T		た (*ta*)	ち (*chi*)	つ (*tsu*)	て (*te*)	と (*to*)
N		な (*na*)	に (*ni*)	ぬ (*nu*)	ね (*ne*)	の (*no*)
H		は (*ha*)	ひ (*hi*)	ふ (*fu*)	へ (*he*)	ほ (*ho*)
M		ま (*ma*)	み (*mi*)	む (*mu*)	め (*me*)	も (*mo*)
Y		や (*ya*)		ゆ (*yu*)		よ (*yo*)
R		ら (*ra*)	り (*ri*)	る (*ru*)	れ (*re*)	ろ (*ro*)
W		わ (*wa*)				を (*wo*)
N				ん (*n*)		

- **Vowel Only**:
  - あ (*a*), い (*i*), う (*u*), え (*e*), お (*o*).
- **Special Sound**:
  - ん (*n*) is the only character that does not follow the consonant + vowel pattern.

Tips for Learning the Hiragana Characters:

1. **Focus on One Row at a Time**:
   Start by memorizing and practicing one row (e.g., the "A" row: あ, い, う, え, お). Use flashcards or a notebook to repeatedly write out each character.

2. **Use Mnemonics**:
   Create a visual or verbal mnemonic for each character to help remember the shape and sound. For example:
   - あ (*a*) resembles a person shouting "Ah!"
   - い (*i*) looks like two parallel lines, as in the number 2 in Roman numerals (II).

3. **Practice Writing and Saying the Characters Aloud**:
   Practice each character with the correct **stroke order** (introduced in the next section) while saying the sound out loud. This helps solidify the connection between visual recognition, writing, and pronunciation.

4. **Review with Common Words**:
   As you progress, try recognizing Hiragana characters in simple Japanese words, such as:

- ○ さくら (*sakura* - cherry blossom)
- ○ すし (*sushi* - sushi)
- ○ やさい (*yasai* - vegetables)

Stroke Order and Writing Practice

Writing Hiragana correctly involves following a specific **stroke order** for each character. This stroke order is designed to make the characters flow naturally and be visually balanced.

Practicing the correct stroke order from the beginning will help your writing look more authentic and readable. Here, we'll break down each row and provide detailed guides on how to form each character.

General Rules for Stroke Order:

1. **Top to Bottom**: Begin writing from the top and work your way down.
2. **Left to Right**: Start each stroke from the left and move to the right where applicable.
3. **Horizontal First, Then Vertical**: For characters that have both horizontal and vertical strokes, the horizontal strokes are written first.

Practice: The "A" Row Characters (あ, い, う, え, お)

Character	Pronunciation	Stroke Order	Writing Practice Tips
あ	*a*		- Start with a **horizontal stroke** on the top. - Add the **vertical line** extending down with a slight curve. - Finally, draw the **curved loop** on the bottom left.
い	*i*		- Draw two short **parallel vertical lines**. The left line should be slightly longer than the right one.
う	*u*		- Begin with a **short downward stroke** that curves inward. - Draw a **second curved line** that extends to the right and loops back.

え	e		- Start with a **small curve** on the left side. - Add the **rightward stroke** and finish with a **looping shape**.
お	o		- Draw a **short curved stroke** on top. - Add a **vertical line** with a curve at the end. - Complete with a **looped stroke** on the bottom left.

Practice: The "Ka" Row Characters (か, き, く, け, こ)

Character	Pronunciation	Stroke Order	Writing Practice Tips
か	*ka*		- Start with the **diagonal stroke** from the top left to bottom right. - Add the **vertical line** with a slight curve at the end. - Finish with the **small horizontal line** in the middle.
き	*ki*		- Draw a **short horizontal line** on top. - Extend a **vertical line** down, crossing the horizontal stroke. - Draw two **short diagonal lines** that intersect the vertical line.
く	*ku*		- Create a **single curved stroke** that starts at the top left and bends downwards to the right.

け	ke		- Draw a **small horizontal stroke**. - Add the **vertical line** with a hook. - End with the **looped stroke** on the left side.
こ	ko		- Create a **single horizontal stroke**. - Add the **shorter horizontal stroke** just below the first one.

Continue practicing each character until the strokes feel natural. As you write, focus on maintaining the correct proportions and spacing.

Pronunciation Guide

Correct pronunciation is essential when learning Hiragana, as it forms the basis for sounding natural when speaking Japanese. Each Hiragana character represents a distinct syllable consisting of a **vowel sound**, a **consonant + vowel combination**, or the single "n" sound.

In this section, we'll cover how to pronounce each Hiragana character clearly and accurately.

Basic Hiragana Pronunciation

To make it easier to follow, here's a breakdown of the basic **Hiragana syllables** and how they are pronounced. The pronunciation guide will use **English approximations** to help you get a sense of each sound.

Hiragana	Romaji	Pronunciation	Example
あ	a	"ah" as in *car*	あめ (*ame* - rain)
い	i	"ee" as in *see*	いぬ (*inu* - dog)
う	u	"oo" as in *food*	うみ (*umi* - sea)
え	e	"eh" as in *met*	えき (*eki* - station)
お	o	"oh" as in *go*	おちゃ (*ocha* - tea)
か	ka	"ka" as in *car*	かさ (*kasa* - umbrella)

き	ki	"kee" as in *key*	き つ ね (*kitsune* - fox)
く	ku	"koo" as in *cool*	く ま (*kuma* - bear)
け	ke	"keh" as in *kept*	け む り (*kemuri* - smoke)
こ	ko	"koh" as in *coat*	こ ど も (*kodomo* - child)

Key Pronunciation Tips:

1. **Vowel Sounds Are Short and Crisp**: Unlike in English, where vowels can be elongated or diphthongized, Japanese vowels are quick and clear. Keep them short and steady.

2. **Consistent Consonants**: Consonants in Japanese remain constant and are not influenced by surrounding vowels. For example, か (*ka*) sounds like "ka" in *car* regardless of what follows it.

3. **The "R" Sound**: The "R" sound in Hiragana (ら, り, る, れ, ろ) is pronounced as a light tap of the tongue against the roof of the mouth, similar to a blend between "L" and "D."

4. **The "N" Sound**: The character ん (*n*) is pronounced like the "n" in *sun*. When it precedes a "b", "m", or "p" sound, it's closer to an "m" sound (e.g., *sanpo* becomes *sampo*).

5. **Small "っ" for Double Consonants**: When you see a small "っ" (called *sokuon*), it indicates a doubled consonant sound, creating a slight pause before pronouncing the consonant.
   - Example: きって (*kitte* - stamp).

Practice Words

Try reading and saying the following words aloud to get used to combining Hiragana sounds:

1. あさ (asa) – Morning
2. すし (sushi) – Sushi
3. せんせい (sensei) – Teacher
4. さくら (sakura) – Cherry Blossom
5. いえ (ie) – House
6. おおきい (ookii) – Big
7. ねこ (neko) – Cat
8. たべる (taberu) – To eat

Keep practicing until you feel comfortable recognizing and pronouncing each character clearly. You can also use flashcards or listen to audio resources for reinforcement.

Key Takeaways

- ❖ Hiragana consists of **46 basic characters**, each representing a unique syllable sound.
- ❖ Mastering the **correct stroke order** is crucial for writing Hiragana accurately and maintaining the flow and balance of each character.
- ❖ Hiragana is used for **grammatical particles**, **native Japanese words**, and **verb/adjective endings**.
- ❖ The pronunciation of each Hiragana syllable should be clear, short, and consistent.
- ❖ Practice regularly with common words to reinforce your understanding of both writing and pronunciation.

Exercises

Exercise 1: Hiragana Identification

Match the following Hiragana characters to their Romaji (romanized) equivalent:

1. あ → ___
2. か → ___
3. し → ___
4. す → ___
5. も → ___
6. ふ → ___
7. わ → ___
8. り → ___
9. ん → ___
10. け → ___

Exercise 2: Write in Hiragana

Write the following words in Hiragana:

1. **Sakura** (cherry blossom): _______________
2. **Inu** (dog): _____________
3. **Gakkou** (school): _____________
4. **Tabe** (to eat): _____________
5. **Neko** (cat): _____________
6. **Sensei** (teacher): _____________

Exercise 3: Hiragana Sentence Construction

Use the Hiragana characters to complete the sentences:

1. 私は_______を食べます。(*I eat sushi.*)
   - Options: あめ, すし, さくら
2. いぬは_______にいます。(*The dog is in the house.*)
   - Options: いえ, ねこ, くま
3. あなたは_______ですか？(*Are you a teacher?*)
   - Options: せんせい, がっこう, ねこ

Exercise 4: Pronunciation Practice

Read the following Hiragana words aloud. Write down the English meanings if you know them:

1. はな
2. さかな
3. こうえん
4. うみ
5. そら

Answer Key

Exercise 1: Hiragana Identification

1. あ → *a*
2. か → *ka*
3. し → *shi*
4. す → *su*
5. も → *mo*
6. ふ → *fu*
7. わ → *wa*
8. り → *ri*
9. ん → *n*
10. け → *ke*

Exercise 2: Write in Hiragana

1. **Sakura:** さくら
2. **Inu:** いぬ
3. **Gakkou:** がっこう
4. **Tabe:** たべ
5. **Neko:** ねこ
6. **Sensei:** せんせい

Exercise 3: Hiragana Sentence Construction

1. 私は**すし**を食べます。(*I eat sushi.*)
2. いぬは**いえ**にいます。(*The dog is in the house.*)
3. あなたは**せんせい**ですか？(*Are you a teacher?*)

Exercise 4: Pronunciation Practice

1. はな (*hana* - flower)
2. さかな (*sakana* - fish)
3. こうえん (*kouen* - park)
4. うみ (*umi* - sea)
5. そら (*sora* - sky)

Chapter 3: Understanding and Writing Katakana

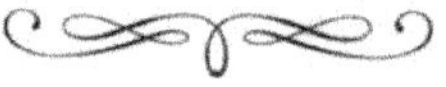

"One language sets you in a corridor for life. Two languages open every door along the way."
– Frank Smith

Now that you've mastered the basics of Hiragana, it's time to introduce the second essential Japanese script: **Katakana**. While Hiragana is used primarily for native Japanese words and grammar, Katakana serves a different purpose. It is used for **foreign words**, **loanwords**, **onomatopoeia**, and **emphasis**. You'll see Katakana often when dealing with modern terms, brand names, and imported vocabulary.

Katakana characters are visually distinct, featuring sharp and angular strokes, unlike the more rounded Hiragana. Because it uses the same set of sounds as Hiragana, learning Katakana will feel somewhat familiar, but you'll need to adjust to the different shapes and stroke orders. Mastering Katakana is essential for reading menus, understanding technical terms, and recognizing many names and places in Japan.

In this chapter, we'll explore the **complete Katakana character set**, learn the correct **stroke order** for writing each character, and practice reading and writing with common **foreign loanwords**. By the end of this chapter, you'll be able to read and write Katakana confidently and apply it to everyday contexts.

Ready to dive into the world of Katakana? Let's begin by looking at the **overview of Katakana characters**!

Overview of Katakana Characters

Katakana, like Hiragana, consists of **46 basic characters** that represent the same syllable sounds. However, Katakana is often used to express **foreign loanwords**, **foreign names**, **scientific terms**, and **emphasis** in written Japanese.

The distinct angular shapes of Katakana make it visually easier to spot, especially in advertisements, product labels, and names written for clarity.

Learning Katakana is crucial because of its role in modern Japanese—many foods, brand names, and technical terms appear almost exclusively in this script. Below is an overview of the complete **Katakana chart** to get you started.

The Basic Katakana Chart

Vowels	A	I	U	E	O
K	カ (ka)	キ (ki)	ク (ku)	ケ (ke)	コ (ko)
S	サ (sa)	シ (shi)	ス (su)	セ (se)	ソ (so)
T	タ (ta)	チ (chi)	ツ (tsu)	テ (te)	ト (to)
N	ナ (na)	ニ (ni)	ヌ (nu)	ネ (ne)	ノ (no)
H	ハ (ha)	ヒ (hi)	フ (fu)	ヘ (he)	ホ (ho)
M	マ (ma)	ミ (mi)	ム (mu)	メ (me)	モ (mo)
Y	ヤ (ya)		ユ (yu)		ヨ (yo)
R	ラ (ra)	リ (ri)	ル (ru)	レ (re)	ロ (ro)
W	ワ (wa)				ヲ (wo)
N			ン (n)		

- **Vowel Only**:
  - ア (a), イ (i), ウ (u), エ (e), オ (o).
- **Special Sound**:
  - ン (n) is the only character that doesn't follow the consonant + vowel pattern, just like in Hiragana.

How to Use Katakana Effectively

Each Katakana character corresponds to a syllable, just like Hiragana. However, it's primarily used for the following purposes:

1. **Foreign Loanwords**:
   - Foreign-origin words (such as those borrowed from English or other languages) are written in Katakana.

- Examples:
  - テレビ (*terebi* - television)
  - コンピュータ (*konpyu-ta* - computer)
  - スマホ (*sumaho* - smartphone)

2. **Foreign Names and Places**:
   - Names of people, countries, and places are often written in Katakana.
   - Examples:
     - ジョン (*Jon* - John)
     - フランス (*Furansu* - France)
     - ニューヨーク (*Nyuu Yooku* - New York)

3. **Technical and Scientific Terms**:
   - Technical terms and scientific vocabulary are often rendered in Katakana.
   - Examples:
     - レーザー (*reezaa* - laser)
     - バクテリア (*bakuteria* - bacteria)

4. **Onomatopoeia**:
   - Katakana is used to write **onomatopoeic sounds** and other sound effects.
   - Examples:
     - ワンワン (*wan wan* - dog barking sound)
     - ピカピカ (*pika pika* - something shiny)

5. **Emphasis**:
   - Katakana can be used for emphasis, similar to how italics are used in English.
   - For instance, using Katakana for native Japanese words can add visual focus in advertisements.

Tips for Memorizing Katakana

1. **Focus on Shapes**:
   Katakana characters are more angular and rigid compared to Hiragana. Notice how many characters have sharp corners and straight lines, making them easier to distinguish.

2. **Use Mnemonics**:
   Like Hiragana, create visual or verbal mnemonics to help remember the shapes and their corresponding sounds.
   - Example: シ (*shi*) looks like a "smiley face" turned sideways.

3. **Group Study**:
   Break down the chart into smaller groups (e.g., study the "K" row separately from the "T" row) to avoid overwhelming yourself.

Practice Reading and Writing Katakana

Just like Hiragana, mastering Katakana involves understanding the **correct stroke order** and practicing writing each character repeatedly until it becomes second nature.

In this section, we'll focus on learning the **stroke order** for each Katakana character. Practicing proper stroke order not only helps with the visual balance of the characters but also ensures that your writing flows naturally.

General Rules for Writing Katakana

1. **Top to Bottom**: Strokes are written from top to bottom.
2. **Left to Right**: When horizontal strokes are present, write from left to right.
3. **Keep Lines Straight**: Unlike the rounded curves of Hiragana, Katakana characters use straighter, sharper lines.

Practice: The "A" Row Characters (ア, イ, ウ, エ, オ)

Character	Pronunciation	Stroke Order	Writing Practice Tips
ア	*a*		- Begin with a **short diagonal stroke** from the top left. - Draw a **horizontal line** across the top. - Finish with a **long vertical stroke** intersecting the horizontal line.
イ	*i*		- Start with a **short diagonal line** on the left. - Draw a **second diagonal line** slightly to the right, extending further down.

ウ	u		- Start with a **small vertical stroke** on the top left. - Draw a **longer curved line** that moves down and to the right. - Finish with a **horizontal stroke** at the bottom right.
エ	e		- Draw a **small horizontal line** on the top left. - Add a **longer horizontal line** extending to the right below the first. - Finish with a **short vertical stroke** intersecting both lines on the right.
オ	o		- Start with a **small vertical line** at the top left. - Draw a **diagonal line** moving down and to the right. - Finish with a **short horizontal stroke** on the bottom left.

Practice: The "Ka" Row Characters (カ, キ, ク, ケ, コ)

Character	Pronunciation	Stroke Order	Writing Practice Tips
カ	ka		- Draw a **short diagonal line** on the top left. - Add a **vertical stroke** from the top right that crosses the diagonal line and curves slightly.
キ	ki		- Draw a **small horizontal line** on top. - Extend a **vertical line** down, crossing the horizontal stroke. - Draw two **short diagonal strokes** intersecting the vertical line.

ク	ku		- Create a **single curved stroke** that starts at the top left and bends downwards to the right.
ケ	ke		- Draw a **short horizontal stroke**. - Add a **vertical line** with a hook. - End with a **looped stroke** on the left side.
コ	ko		- Create a **single horizontal stroke**. - Add the **shorter horizontal stroke** just below the first one.

Continue Practicing Each Character

As you practice writing each character, focus on maintaining the proper proportions and spacing between the strokes. Repetition is key—write out each character **10–15 times** until it feels comfortable. Use **Katakana practice sheets**, if possible, to help guide your writing.

Reading Practice with Simple Words

Try reading the following Katakana words, which are commonly used in Japanese:

1. **コンピュータ** (*konpyu-ta*) – Computer
2. **バナナ** (*banana*) – Banana
3. **テーブル** (*te-buru*) – Table
4. **テレビ** (*terebi*) – Television
5. **ホテル** (*hoteru*) – Hotel

Recognizing Katakana will take some time, but with regular practice, you'll be able to read these words fluently and identify similar patterns in more complex terms.

Common Foreign Loan Words

One of the primary uses of Katakana in Japanese is to represent **foreign loanwords** (also called *gairaigo*). These are words borrowed from other languages—mostly from English—and adapted to the Japanese sound system using Katakana characters.

Because they retain the original foreign pronunciation as closely as possible, knowing Katakana is essential for reading and understanding these terms.

Learning common Katakana words will build your vocabulary and make navigating menus, signs, and product labels much easier.

Let's look at some popular foreign loanwords that are frequently used in daily Japanese.

Basic Foreign Loanwords in Katakana

Below is a list of commonly used Katakana words, along with their English equivalents and pronunciation guides.

Katakana	Romaji	English	Pronunciation Guide
テレビ	*terebi*	Television	"teh-reh-bee"
コンピュータ	*konpyu-ta*	Computer	"kohn-pyu-ta"
ホテル	*hoteru*	Hotel	"ho-teh-ru"
レストラン	*resutoran*	Restaurant	"res-tor-an"
バス	*basu*	Bus	"bah-su"
トイレ	*toire*	Toilet	"toi-reh"
サンドイッチ	*sandoicchi*	Sandwich	"san-do-icchi"
コーヒー	*ko-hi-*	Coffee	"koh-hee"
チーズ	*chi-zu*	Cheese	"chee-zu"
パン	*pan*	Bread (from Portuguese)	"pan"
ハンバーガー	*hanba-ga-*	Hamburger	"han-baa-gaa"
メニュー	*menyu-*	Menu	"men-yuu"

サラダ	*sarada*	Salad	"sa-ra-da"
スマホ	*sumaho*	Smartphone	"su-ma-ho"
シャツ	*shatsu*	Shirt	"sha-tsu"
ケーキ	*ke-ki*	Cake	"keh-kee"

Understanding Katakana Adaptations

Since Japanese has a limited set of syllables, foreign words are often adapted to fit the Japanese sound system, resulting in slight changes to the pronunciation. Here are a few points to keep in mind:

1. **No Consonant Clusters**:
   - English words with consonant clusters (e.g., *spring*) are split into separate syllables in Japanese (e.g., スプリング - *su-pu-rin-gu*).
2. **Extended Vowels**:
   - Long vowels in foreign words are marked with a dash (ー) in Katakana.
   - Example: コーヒー (*ko-hi-*) for "coffee"
3. **Simplified Sounds**:
   - Certain English sounds, like "th" or "v," don't exist in Japanese, so they are replaced with similar sounds.
   - Example: *th* in *theater* becomes シアター (*shi-a-ta-*).

Practice Reading Common Foreign Loan Words

Try reading the following Katakana loanwords aloud. Pay attention to the rhythm and pronunciation.

1. **バイク** (*baiku*) – Bike
2. **アイスクリーム** (*aisukuri-mu*) – Ice Cream
3. **スプーン** (*supu-n*) – Spoon
4. **ゲーム** (*ge-mu*) – Game
5. **テレビジョン** (*terebijon*) – Television

Recognizing loanwords will help you pick up on common terms in Japanese texts, menus, and everyday communication.

As you continue to practice, you'll become more familiar with how these words are adapted and pronounced.

Key Takeaways

❖ **Katakana** is primarily used for **foreign loanwords**, **names**, **scientific terms**, and **emphasis** in Japanese.

❖ Each Katakana character represents a syllable, just like Hiragana, but with distinct, sharp strokes.

❖ Understanding Katakana is essential for reading **imported words**, **product labels**, and **technical terms**.

❖ Foreign words are often adapted to the Japanese sound system, which can result in slight changes in pronunciation (e.g., "coffee" becomes コーヒー).

❖ Learning Katakana will make it easier to navigate menus, advertisements, and everyday written materials in Japan.

Exercises

Exercise 1: Katakana Identification
Match each Katakana character with its Romaji equivalent:

1. テ → ___
2. コ → ___
3. サ → ___
4. ハ → ___
5. ン → ___
6. メ → ___
7. ト → ___
8. シ → ___
9. ヒ → ___
10. ラ → ___

Exercise 2: Write in Katakana
Convert the following foreign words into Katakana:

1. **Coffee**: _______________
2. **Pizza**: _______________
3. **Hotel**: _______________
4. **Sandwich**: _______________
5. **Taxi**: _______________

Exercise 3: Reading Foreign Loanwords
Read the following Katakana words and write down their English equivalents:

1. スマホ
2. パン
3. サラダ
4. アイスクリーム
5. コンピュータ

Exercise 4: Mixed Script Sentence

Complete the sentence below using the appropriate Katakana word:

1. 私は＿＿＿＿＿を飲みます。 (*I drink coffee.*)

   ○ Options: バス, コーヒー, テーブル

2. あなたは＿＿＿＿＿へ行きますか？ (*Are you going to the hotel?*)

   ○ Options: サラダ, ホテル, ゲーム

3. これは＿＿＿＿＿ですか？ (*Is this a sandwich?*)

   ○ Options: パン, メニュー, サンドイッチ

Answer Key

Exercise 1: Katakana Identification

1. テ → *te*
2. コ → *ko*
3. サ → *sa*
4. ハ → *ha*
5. ン → *n*
6. メ → *me*
7. ト → *to*
8. シ → *shi*
9. ヒ → *hi*
10. ラ → *ra*

Exercise 2: Write in Katakana

1. **Coffee**: コーヒー
2. **Pizza**: ピザ
3. **Hotel**: ホテル
4. **Sandwich**: サンドイッチ
5. **Taxi**: タクシー

Exercise 3: Reading Foreign Loanwords

1. スマホ – Smartphone
2. パン – Bread
3. サラダ – Salad
4. アイスクリーム – Ice Cream
5. コンピュータ – Computer

Exercise 4: Mixed Script Sentence

1. 私は**コーヒー**を飲みます。(*I drink coffee.*)
2. あなたは**ホテル**へ行きますか？(*Are you going to the hotel?*)
3. これは**サンドイッチ**ですか？(*Is this a sandwich?*)

Chapter 4: Getting Started with Basic Kanji

"Learning is a treasure that will follow its owner everywhere."
– Chinese Proverb

Welcome to the world of **Kanji**—the most complex and intriguing part of the Japanese writing system. Kanji characters, borrowed from Chinese, are unique in that they convey **meanings** rather than just sounds. Each Kanji character represents an idea, and understanding how they function will unlock a deeper comprehension of the Japanese language.

For beginners, Kanji can seem overwhelming because of the sheer number of characters and their complex shapes. However, the key to mastering Kanji is to start with the **basics** and build your knowledge step-by-step. In this chapter, you will learn about the **core elements** of Kanji, called **radicals**, and master 50 essential characters that are commonly used in daily life.

Each Kanji character is made up of smaller components called **radicals**, which serve as the building blocks for the larger characters. By learning these radicals first, you'll gain the ability to decipher new Kanji more easily and make connections between related characters. This chapter will guide you through the **most frequently used radicals** and then move on to 50 basic Kanji that will be useful for reading simple texts and forming essential words.

By the end of this chapter, you'll be able to recognize and write some of the most common Kanji characters, understand their meanings, and see how they fit into Japanese sentences. Let's start by breaking down the building blocks of Kanji: **the radicals**.

Introduction to Kanji Radicals

Before diving into individual Kanji characters, it's important to understand the **building blocks** that make up these complex symbols. These components are called **radicals** (*bushu* in Japanese), and they form the foundation of nearly every Kanji character.

What Are Kanji Radicals?

A radical is a smaller element within a Kanji character that contributes to its **overall meaning** or **category**. Think of radicals as the roots of a tree—each one connects to a group of related Kanji that share similar meanings or origins.

- For example, the radical 水 (*mizu*), meaning "water," appears in Kanji characters related to liquids, such as 海 (*umi* - sea) and 池 (*ike* - pond).

In total, there are over **200 radicals**, but don't worry! You only need to know around **30-40 key radicals** to unlock the most basic Kanji.

Common Kanji Radicals You Should Know

Below is a list of **10 essential radicals** to get started. You'll see these radicals frequently in many beginner-level Kanji; recognizing them will make the learning process smoother.

Radical	Name	Meaning	Example Kanji	Kanji Meaning
人	*nin / hito*	Person/Human	体 (*karada*)	Body
口	*kuchi*	Mouth	吃 (*kitsu*)	To stutter
木	*ki*	Tree/Wood	林 (*hayashi*)	Forest
土	*tsuchi*	Earth/Soil	地 (*chi*)	Ground
火	*hi*	Fire	炎 (*honoo*)	Flame
水	*mizu*	Water	海 (*umi*)	Sea
女	*onna*	Woman/Female	妹 (*imouto*)	Younger sister
日	*hi*	Sun/Day	明 (*aka*)	Bright
食	*shoku*	Food/Eat	飲 (*nomu*)	To drink
金	*kane*	Gold/Metal/Money	銀 (*gin*)	Silver

Why Learn Radicals First?

1. **Understanding Structure**:
   Each radical has a meaning, and when combined with other radicals, they form more complex characters. By learning radicals, you'll start seeing patterns and connections between different Kanji.

2. **Improving Memory**:
   Rather than memorizing every stroke of a complex Kanji, breaking it down into its component radicals makes it easier to remember.

3. **Enhancing Recognition**:
   When you encounter unfamiliar Kanji, recognizing the radicals within can give you clues to its meaning, making reading less intimidating.

How Radicals Shape Kanji Meaning

Radicals often give **hints** about the character's overall meaning or pronunciation. Let's take a look at a few examples:

1. 木 **(Tree Radical)**:

   - 森 (*mori* - forest): The Kanji 森 is made up of three 木 characters stacked together, symbolizing many trees collectively forming a forest.

   - 校 (*kou* - school): The 木 radical in this character suggests a "gathering place," similar to a tree's roots.

2. 水 **(Water Radical)**:

   - 河 (*kawa* - river): The Kanji for river contains the water radical on the left, symbolizing its connection to water.

   - 汁 (*shiru* - soup): Similarly, 汁 uses the water radical to suggest a liquid substance.

3. 火 **(Fire Radical)**:

   - 焼 (*yaki* - to burn): The fire radical adds the sense of heat or burning to the character's meaning.

50 Basic Kanji for Daily Use

These 50 basic Kanji are a great starting point because they appear frequently in daily contexts, such as signs, menus, and basic texts. Mastering these characters will greatly enhance your ability to read and understand simple Japanese.

Each Kanji character in this list will be presented along with its **meaning**, **readings** (both *On'yomi* and *Kun'yomi*), and **example words** to show how it's used.

Kanji List: 50 Essential Characters

Kanji	Meaning	On'yomi	Kun'yomi	Example Word	Meaning of Example
日	Sun/Day	*nichi*	*hi*	日曜日 (*nichiyoubi*)	Sunday
月	Moon/Month	*getsu*	*tsuki*	月 (*tsuki*)	Moon
火	Fire	*ka*	*hi*	火山 (*kazan*)	Volcano
水	Water	*sui*	*mizu*	水 (*mizu*)	Water
木	Tree/Wood	*moku*	*ki*	木 (*ki*)	Tree
金	Gold/Money	*kin*	*kane*	お金 (*okane*)	Money
土	Earth/Soil	*do*	*tsuchi*	土地 (*tochi*)	Land
人	Person/Human	*jin*	*hito*	日本人 (*nihonjin*)	Japanese person
口	Mouth	*kou*	*kuchi*	入口 (*iriguchi*)	Entrance
目	Eye	*moku*	*me*	目 (*me*)	Eye
子	Child	*shi*	*ko*	子供 (*kodomo*)	Child
女	Woman/Female	*jo*	*onna*	女 (*onna*)	Woman
男	Man/Male	*dan*	*otoko*	男 (*otoko*)	Man
山	Mountain	*san*	*yama*	山 (*yama*)	Mountain
川	River	*sen*	*kawa*	川 (*kawa*)	River

田	Rice Field	*den*	*ta*	田んぼ (*tanbo*)	Rice Field
車	Car	*sha*	*kuruma*	車 (*kuruma*)	Car
学	Study/ School	*gaku*	*manabu*	学校 (*gakkou*)	School
校	School/ Exam	*kou*	—	学校 (*gakkou*)	School
生	Life/Birth	*sei*	*ikiru*	先生 (*sensei*)	Teacher
先	Before/ Previous	*sen*	*saki*	先生 (*sensei*)	Teacher
何	What	*ka*	*nani*	何 (*nani*)	What
名	Name/Fame	*mei*	*na*	名前 (*namae*)	Name
気	Spirit/ Feeling	*ki*	—	天気 (*tenki*)	Weather
休	Rest	*kyuu*	*yasumu*	休み (*yasumi*)	Break/Holiday
小	Small	*shou*	*chiisai*	小さい (*chiisai*)	Small
大	Big	*dai*	*ookii*	大きい (*ookii*)	Big
中	Middle/ Inside	*chuu*	*naka*	中 (*naka*)	Inside
上	Up/Above	*jou*	*ue*	上 (*ue*)	Above/Up
下	Down/Below	*ka*	*shita*	下 (*shita*)	Below/Down

左	Left	*sa*	*hidari*	左 (*hidari*)	Left
右	Right	*u*	*migi*	右 (*migi*)	Right
前	Front/Before	*zen*	*mae*	前 (*mae*)	Front
後	After/Behind	*go*	*ushiro*	後 (*ushiro*)	Behind
天	Heaven/Sky	*ten*	*ame*	天気 (*tenki*)	Weather
雨	Rain	*u*	*ame*	雨 (*ame*)	Rain
電	Electricity	*den*	—	電話 (*denwa*)	Telephone
話	Talk/Speak	*wa*	*hanasu*	話す (*hanasu*)	To speak
見	See/Look	*ken*	*miru*	見る (*miru*)	To see
書	Write	*sho*	*kaku*	書く (*kaku*)	To write
食	Eat	*shoku*	*taberu*	食べる (*taberu*)	To eat
飲	Drink	*in*	*nomu*	飲む (*nomu*)	To drink
時	Time/Hour	*ji*	*toki*	時間 (*jikan*)	Time
年	Year	*nen*	*toshi*	年 (*toshi*)	Year
友	Friend	*yuu*	*tomo*	友達 (*tomodachi*)	Friend
道	Road/Way	*dou*	*michi*	道 (*michi*)	Road

Reading and Writing Practice

Now that you've been introduced to 50 essential Kanji, it's time to practice writing and reading some of these characters.

Below is a set of commonly used Kanji from the list for focused practice. For each character, I'll include the **stroke order**, **readings**, and **example words**.

Kanji Practice Table 1: Basic Kanji Characters

Kanji	Meaning	On'yomi	Kun'yomi	Example Word	Example Meaning
日	Sun/Day	*nichi*	*hi*	日曜日 (*nichiyoubi*)	Sunday
月	Moon/Month	*getsu*	*tsuki*	月 (*tsuki*)	Moon
木	Tree/Wood	*moku*	*ki*	木 (*ki*)	Tree
山	Mountain	*san*	*yama*	山 (*yama*)	Mountain
口	Mouth	*kou*	*kuchi*	口 (*kuchi*)	Mouth
人	Person	*jin*	*hito*	人 (*hito*)	Person
火	Fire	*ka*	*hi*	火 (*hi*)	Fire
水	Water	*sui*	*mizu*	水 (*mizu*)	Water
田	Rice Field	*den*	*ta*	田んぼ (*tanbo*)	Rice Field
車	Car	*sha*	*kuruma*	車 (*kuruma*)	Car

Kanji Practice Table 2: Kanji for Time and Numbers

Kanji	Meaning	On'yomi	Kun'yomi	Example Word	Example Meaning
時	Time/Hour	*ji*	*toki*	時間 (*jikan*)	Time/Duration
年	Year	*nen*	*toshi*	年 (*toshi*)	Year
月	Month/Moon	*getsu*	*tsuki*	月 (*tsuki*)	Month
日	Day	*nichi*	*hi*	日 (*hi*)	Day
先	Previous	*sen*	*saki*	先生 (*sensei*)	Teacher (lit. "Previous Birth")
名	Name	*mei*	*na*	名前 (*namae*)	Name

Key Takeaways

❖ **Kanji are logographic characters** that convey meanings rather than just sounds.

❖ Each Kanji character is made up of **radicals**, which are the building blocks that form the character and influence its meaning.

❖ Learning basic **Kanji radicals** helps simplify the process of recognizing, reading, and remembering complex characters.

❖ Familiarize yourself with the **stroke order** for each Kanji to ensure proper writing technique and legibility.

❖ Focus on mastering **common Kanji used in daily life**, such as those for numbers, basic nouns, and directions.

Exercises

Exercise 1: Kanji Meaning Matching
Match the Kanji to its English meaning:

1. 人 → __
2. 火 → __
3. 口 → __
4. 山 → __
5. 木 → __
6. 水 → __
7. 田 → __
8. 車 → __
9. 月 → __
10. 金 → __

Options:
A. Water

B. Fire

C. Mountain

D. Mouth

E. Tree

F. Person

G. Car

H. Moon/Month

I. Rice Field

J. Gold/Money

Exercise 2: Write the Kanji
Write the following English words using the correct Kanji characters:

1. **Water:** _______________
2. **Fire:** _______________
3. **Tree:** _______________
4. **Car:** _______________
5. **Sun/Day:** _______________

6. **Mountain**: _______________

7. **Mouth**: _______________

8. **Gold/Money**: _______________

Exercise 3: Read and Translate

Read the following Kanji phrases and write down their meanings:

1. 日曜日
2. 火山
3. 田んぼ
4. 水車
5. 木曜日
6. 学校
7. 人口
8. 月曜日

Exercise 4: Sentence Practice

Fill in the blanks with the correct Kanji character based on the English word in parentheses:

1. 私は (*fire*) を見ます。
2. 田んぼは (*water*) でいっぱいです。
3. 今日は (*Sunday*) ですか？
4. 山の上に (*tree*) があります。
5. 私は (*person*) です。

Answer Key

Exercise 1: Kanji Meaning Matching

1. 人 → F. Person
2. 火 → B. Fire
3. 口 → D. Mouth
4. 山 → C. Mountain
5. 木 → E. Tree
6. 水 → A. Water
7. 田 → I. Rice Field
8. 車 → G. Car
9. 月 → H. Moon/Month
10. 金 → J. Gold/Money

Exercise 2: Write the Kanji

1. **Water:** 水
2. **Fire:** 火
3. **Tree:** 木
4. **Car:** 車
5. **Sun/Day:** 日
6. **Mountain:** 山
7. **Mouth:** 口
8. **Gold/Money:** 金

Exercise 3: Read and Translate

1. 日曜日 (*nichiyoubi*) – Sunday
2. 火山 (*kazan*) – Volcano
3. 田んぼ (*tanbo*) – Rice Field
4. 水車 (*suisha*) – Waterwheel
5. 木曜日 (*mokuyoubi*) – Thursday
6. 学校 (*gakkou*) – School

7. 人口 (*jinkou*) – Population

8. 月曜日 (*getsuyoubi*) – Monday

Exercise 4: Sentence Practice

1. 私は火を見ます。(*I see fire.*)

2. 田んぼは水でいっぱいです。(*The rice field is full of water.*)

3. 今日は日曜日ですか？(*Is today Sunday?*)

4. 山の上に木があります。(*There is a tree on top of the mountain.*)

5. 私は人です。(*I am a person.*)

Chapter 5: Combining Hiragana, Katakana, and Kanji

"Language is the road map of a culture. It tells you where its people come from and where they are going."
— Rita Mae Brown

Up to this point, you've learned how to read and write **Hiragana, Katakana**, and some **basic Kanji**. Now, it's time to take your skills to the next level by combining these scripts into **complete words and phrases**. Japanese writing doesn't use one script exclusively; instead, Hiragana, Katakana, and Kanji are blended together in sentences to convey meaning more effectively.

Understanding how these scripts work together is a crucial step toward becoming comfortable with reading and writing in Japanese. The interplay between the scripts helps clarify the context, meaning, and pronunciation of each word, making Japanese more readable and expressive.

In this chapter, we'll explore how to build simple words and phrases by **combining all three scripts**. You'll learn when to use each script within a word or sentence, see how they naturally blend in various contexts, and practice reading and writing sentences that incorporate Hiragana, Katakana, and Kanji.

By the end of this chapter, you'll be able to construct basic sentences, recognize common patterns, and read simple Japanese texts with confidence. Let's start by creating some **simple words and phrases** using the skills you've acquired so far!

Building Simple Words and Phrases

Now that you've mastered the individual scripts of **Hiragana, Katakana**, and **Kanji**, it's time to see how they come together to form complete words and sentences in Japanese.

Typically, Hiragana is used for grammatical elements like particles and verb endings, while Kanji represents the core meanings of words, and Katakana is used for foreign loanwords and names.

Let's start by exploring how these scripts work together in some basic words and phrases.

Combining Hiragana and Kanji

In many words, Kanji is used for the **root** of the word, and Hiragana is used for the **inflection** (such as verb endings or particles). Here are a few common examples:

Japanese	Romaji	Meaning	Script Breakdown
見ます	*mimasu*	To see	見 (Kanji for "see") + ます

			(Hiragana for polite verb ending)
食べます	*tabemasu*	To eat	食 (Kanji for "eat") + べます (Hiragana verb ending, root is 食べる "taberu")
行きます	*ikimasu*	To go	行 (Kanji for "go") + きます (Hiragana for polite verb ending)
学校	*gakkou*	School	学 (Kanji for "study/learning") + 校 (Kanji for "school")
大きい	*ookii*	Big	大 (Kanji for "big") + きい (Hiragana adjective ending)

In each of these examples, the Kanji conveys the **core meaning** of the word, while Hiragana adds **grammatical details** like tense or conjugation.

Combining Katakana with Hiragana and Kanji

Katakana is typically used for foreign words, names, or technical terms. Let's look at some examples of words and phrases where Katakana is integrated:

Japanese	Romaji	Meaning	Script Breakdown
テレビを見ます	*terebi o mimasu*	I watch TV	テレビ (Katakana for "television") + 見ます (Kanji + Hiragana for "watch")
コーヒーを飲みます	*ko-hi- o nomimasu*	I drink coffee	コーヒー (Katakana for "coffee") + 飲みます (Kanji + Hiragana for "drink")
パンを食べます	*pan o tabemasu*	I eat bread	パン (Katakana for "bread") + 食べます (Kanji + Hiragana for "eat")
ジョンさんは日本人です	*Jon-san wa nihonjin desu*	John is Japanese	ジョン (Katakana for "John") + 日本人 (Kanji for "Japanese person")

As you can see, Katakana is often used for foreign words or names, while Kanji and Hiragana are used for native Japanese words and grammatical markers.

Basic Sentence Construction

Japanese sentence structure is typically **Subject-Object-Verb** (SOV). Here are a few simple sentences that combine all three scripts:

1. 私は学校へ行きます。

   - *Watashi wa gakkou e ikimasu.*
   - **Meaning**: I go to school.
   - **Breakdown**: 私 (Kanji for "I") + は (Hiragana particle) + 学校 (Kanji for "school") + へ (Hiragana particle) + 行きます (Kanji + Hiragana for "to go")

2. 彼はテニスをします。

   - *Kare wa tenisu o shimasu.*
   - **Meaning**: He plays tennis.
   - **Breakdown**: 彼 (Kanji for "he") + は (Hiragana particle) + テニス (Katakana for "tennis") + を (Hiragana particle) + します (Hiragana verb "to do")

3. マリアさんは日本語を勉強します。

   - *Maria-san wa nihongo o benkyou shimasu.*
   - **Meaning**: Maria studies Japanese.
   - **Breakdown**: マリア (Katakana for "Maria") + さん (Hiragana for respectful address) + 日本語 (Kanji for "Japanese language") + を (Hiragana particle) + 勉強 (Kanji for "study") + します (Hiragana verb for "to do")

This is how **Hiragana**, **Katakana**, and **Kanji** naturally blend together in real-world sentences.

Practice Reading and Writing Mixed Scripts

Let's practice constructing sentences and reading words that use a combination of **Hiragana**, **Katakana**, and **Kanji**. This section will focus on building familiarity with switching between the scripts and understanding how they work together in real Japanese text.

Practice Words Using Mixed Scripts

Let's start with some basic vocabulary and phrases that combine all three scripts. Try reading each word aloud, identifying the role of each script, and then writing them out.

Japanese	Romaji	Meaning	Script Breakdown
テーブルの上に本があります。	*te-buru no ue ni hon ga arimasu.*	There is a book on the table.	テーブル (Katakana for "table") + の (Hiragana particle) + 上

			(Kanji for "up") + に (Hiragana particle) + 本 (Kanji for "book") + が (Hiragana particle) + あ り ま す (Hiragana verb ending)
私は映画を見 ます。	*watashi wa eiga o mimasu.*	I watch a movie.	私 (Kanji for "I") + は (Hiragana particle) + 映 画 (Kanji for "movie") + を (Hiragana particle) + 見 ま す (Kanji + Hiragana for "to watch")
これは日本の レストランで す。	*kore wa nihon no resutoran desu.*	This is a Japanese restaurant.	これ (Hiragana for "this") + は (Hiragana particle) + 日本 (Kanji for "Japan") + の (Hiragana particle) + レ ストラン (Katakana for "restaurant") + です (Hiragana for "is")
猫はベッドの 下にいます。	*neko wa beddo no shita ni imasu.*	The cat is under the bed.	猫 (Kanji for "cat") + は (Hiragana particle) + ベ ッド (Katakana for "bed") + の (Hiragana particle) + 下 (Kanji for "under") + に (Hiragana particle) + います (Hiragana for "is")

Key Takeaways

❖ Japanese uses a combination of **Hiragana**, **Katakana**, and **Kanji** in the same sentence to create clarity and add meaning.

❖ **Hiragana** is used for **particles**, **verb endings**, and **native Japanese words**.

❖ **Katakana** is used for **foreign loanwords**, **names**, and **technical terms**.

❖ **Kanji** represents the **core meaning** of words, such as nouns, verbs, and adjectives.

❖ Understanding how these scripts work together is essential for reading real Japanese sentences and texts.

❖ Practice combining all three scripts to build your fluency in recognizing words and sentence patterns.

Exercises

Exercise 1: Script Identification
For each word below, identify which script(s) are used (Hiragana, Katakana, or Kanji):

1. 猫
2. テレビ
3. 学生
4. コーヒー
5. 学校
6. すし
7. 車
8. サンドイッチ
9. 魚
10. 先生

Options:

- Hiragana
- Katakana
- Kanji
- Mixed (Hiragana + Kanji)

Exercise 2: Translate the Sentence
Translate the following mixed-script sentences into English:

1. 私はすしを食べます。
2. ジョンさんは日本に行きます。
3. 学生は本を読みます。
4. 今日は月曜日です。
5. あなたはコーヒーを飲みますか？

Exercise 3: Fill in the Blanks

Complete the sentences below by choosing the correct word in Katakana, Hiragana, or Kanji:

1. 私は＿＿＿＿＿＿を食べます。 (*I eat sushi.*)

   ○ Options: すし (Hiragana), 犬 (Kanji), サラダ (Katakana)

2. これは＿＿＿＿＿＿ですか？ (*Is this a book?*)

   ○ Options: 車 (Kanji), 本 (Kanji), コーヒー (Katakana)

3. 学生は＿＿＿＿＿＿に行きます。 (*The student goes to the library.*)

   ○ Options: 学校 (Kanji), 本 (Kanji), 図書館 (Kanji)

4. 彼は＿＿＿＿＿＿を飲みます。 (*He drinks tea.*)

   ○ Options: お茶 (Hiragana + Kanji), パン (Katakana), 猫 (Kanji)

5. あなたは＿＿＿＿＿＿を読みますか？ (*Do you read books?*)

   ○ Options: 魚 (Kanji), 本 (Kanji), いぬ (Hiragana)

Exercise 4: Sentence Construction Practice

Create a sentence using each of the words below, combining them with particles and verb endings as necessary:

1. 本 (*hon* - book)
2. テレビ (*terebi* - TV)
3. 見ます (*mimasu* - to see)
4. 学校 (*gakkou* - school)
5. 月曜日 (*getsuyoubi* - Monday)

Answer Key

Exercise 1: Script Identification

1. 猫 → Kanji
2. テレビ → Katakana
3. 学生 → Kanji
4. コーヒー → Katakana
5. 学校 → Kanji
6. すし → Hiragana
7. 車 → Kanji
8. サンドイッチ → Katakana
9. 魚 → Kanji
10. 先生 → Kanji

Exercise 2: Translate the Sentence

1. 私はすしを食べます。
   - *Watashi wa sushi o tabemasu.*
   - **Meaning**: I eat sushi.
2. ジョンさんは日本に行きます。
   - *Jon-san wa Nihon ni ikimasu.*
   - **Meaning**: John goes to Japan.
3. 学生は本を読みます。
   - *Gakusei wa hon o yomimasu.*
   - **Meaning**: The student reads a book.
4. 今日は月曜日です。
   - *Kyou wa getsuyoubi desu.*
   - **Meaning**: Today is Monday.
5. あなたはコーヒーを飲みますか？
   - *Anata wa ko-hi- o nomimasu ka?*
   - **Meaning**: Do you drink coffee?

Exercise 3: Fill in the Blanks

1. 私は**すし**を食べます。(*I eat sushi.*)
2. これは**本**ですか？(*Is this a book?*)
3. 学生は**図書館**に行きます。(*The student goes to the library.*)
4. 彼は**お茶**を飲みます。(*He drinks tea.*)
5. あなたは**本**を読みますか？(*Do you read books?*)

Exercise 4: Sentence Construction Practice

1. **本**: 私は本を読みます。(*Watashi wa hon o yomimasu. - I read a book.*)
2. **テレビ**: 彼はテレビを見ます。(*Kare wa terebi o mimasu. - He watches TV.*)
3. **見ます**: 学生は映画を見ます。(*Gakusei wa eiga o mimasu. - The student watches a movie.*)
4. **学校**: 私は学校へ行きます。(*Watashi wa gakkou e ikimasu. - I go to school.*)
5. **月曜日**: 月曜日に学校へ行きます。(*Getsuyoubi ni gakkou e ikimasu. - I go to school on Monday.*)

Chapter 6: Everyday Words and Basic Sentence Patterns

"One language sets you in a corridor for life. Two languages open every door along the way."
– Frank Smith

With your understanding of the Japanese writing system and basic vocabulary, it's time to focus on building a **working set of words and phrases** that you can use in **everyday conversations**. This chapter will introduce essential Japanese words that you'll need for common topics like greetings, family, time, and directions. Once you've built up this foundational vocabulary, we'll move on to creating **simple sentence patterns** using these words.

Knowing individual words is helpful, but the real power of language comes when you can **put them together into sentences**. This chapter will teach you how to form basic sentences using the **Subject-Object-Verb (SOV)** structure, ask simple questions, and use some common phrases to navigate day-to-day situations.

By the end of this chapter, you'll have the tools to introduce yourself, talk about your daily routine, ask for basic information, and express your needs confidently in Japanese. Let's start by building a collection of **useful everyday words**!

Useful Words in Japanese

When learning a new language, having a set of **core vocabulary words** is crucial for building confidence in everyday communication.

In this section, you'll find a list of **basic words and phrases** that are essential for daily use. These words cover common topics such as **greetings**, **people**, **places**, and **time** to help you express yourself in various situations.

1. Greetings and Polite Expressions

Japanese	Romaji	Meaning
こんにちは	*konnichiwa*	Hello / Good afternoon
おはようございます	*ohayou gozaimasu*	Good morning
こんばんは	*konbanwa*	Good evening

さようなら	*sayounara*	Goodbye
おやすみなさい	*oyasuminasai*	Good night
ありがとう	*arigatou*	Thank you
すみません	*sumimasen*	Excuse me / I'm sorry
はい	*hai*	Yes
いいえ	*iie*	No
どうぞ	*douzo*	Please / Go ahead
いらっしゃいませ	*irasshaimase*	Welcome (in stores)

2. Talking About People and Family

Japanese	Romaji	Meaning
私	*watashi*	I / Me
あなた	*anata*	You
彼	*kare*	He / Him
彼女	*kanojo*	She / Her
家族	*kazoku*	Family
母	*haha*	Mother
父	*chichi*	Father
兄	*ani*	Older brother

姉	*ane*	Older sister
弟	*otouto*	Younger brother
妹	*imouto*	Younger sister
友達	*tomodachi*	Friend

3. Places Around Town

Japanese	**Romaji**	**Meaning**
学校	*gakkou*	School
図書館	*toshokan*	Library
銀行	*ginkou*	Bank
公園	*kouen*	Park
病院	*byouin*	Hospital
郵便局	*yuubinkyoku*	Post office
駅	*eki*	Station
レストラン	*resutoran*	Restaurant
スーパー	*su-pa-*	Supermarket
喫茶店	*kissaten*	Cafe
家	*ie*	House / Home

4. Time and Days of the Week

Japanese	Romaji	Meaning
時間	*jikan*	Time
今日	*kyou*	Today
明日	*ashita*	Tomorrow
昨日	*kinou*	Yesterday
月曜日	*getsuyoubi*	Monday
火曜日	*kayoubi*	Tuesday
水曜日	*suiyoubi*	Wednesday
木曜日	*mokuyoubi*	Thursday
金曜日	*kinyoubi*	Friday
土曜日	*doyoubi*	Saturday
日曜日	*nichiyoubi*	Sunday
週末	*shuumatsu*	Weekend

5. Common Verbs

Japanese	Romaji	Meaning
行く	*iku*	To go
来る	*kuru*	To come

見る	*miru*	To see
食べる	*taberu*	To eat
飲む	*nomu*	To drink
読む	*yomu*	To read
書く	*kaku*	To write
会う	*au*	To meet
買う	*kau*	To buy
話す	*hanasu*	To speak
聞く	*kiku*	To listen

6. Numbers (1-10)

Japanese	Romaji	Meaning
一	*ichi*	One
二	*ni*	Two
三	*san*	Three
四	*yon / shi*	Four
五	*go*	Five
六	*roku*	Six
七	*nana / shichi*	Seven

八	*hachi*	Eight
九	*kyuu / ku*	Nine
十	*juu*	Ten

Creating Simple Sentences

Now that you have a collection of useful words, let's learn how to combine them into **simple sentences** using basic sentence patterns. Japanese sentence structure typically follows a **Subject-Object-Verb (SOV)** pattern, and particles like は (*wa*), を (*wo*), and に (*ni*) help clarify the relationships between the words.

We'll cover the following patterns:

1. **Subject は Object を Verb.**

   - 私は本を読みます。(*Watashi wa hon o yomimasu.*) – I read a book.

   - 彼女はりんごを食べます。(*Kanojo wa ringo o tabemasu.*) – She eats an apple.

2. **Subject は Place に 行きます (to go).**

   - 彼は学校に行きます。(*Kare wa gakkou ni ikimasu.*) – He goes to school.

   - 私は図書館に行きます。(*Watashi wa toshokan ni ikimasu.*) – I go to the library.

3. **Subject は Time に Verb.**

   - 私は月曜日に映画を見ます。(*Watashi wa getsuyoubi ni eiga o mimasu.*) – I watch a movie on Monday.

   - 学生は午後に勉強します。(*Gakusei wa gogo ni benkyou shimasu.*) – The student studies in the afternoon.

Key Takeaways

- ❖ Building a **core vocabulary** of everyday words is essential for basic communication. Focus on learning words for greetings, family members, places, time, and common verbs.

- ❖ Japanese sentences typically follow a **Subject-Object-Verb (SOV)** structure, which is different from English's Subject-Verb-Object (SVO) structure.

- ❖ Use **particles** like は (*wa*), を (*wo*), and に (*ni*) to indicate the relationships between words in a sentence:
    - ➢ は marks the **subject** of the sentence.
    - ➢ を marks the **direct object**.
    - ➢ に indicates a **destination** or **point in time**.

- ❖ Practice forming basic sentences using these patterns:
    - ➢ **Subject は Object を Verb**: 私は本を読みます。(*I read a book.*)
    - ➢ **Subject は Place に 行きます**: 彼は学校に行きます。(*He goes to school.*)
    - ➢ **Subject は Time に Verb**: 学生は午後に勉強します。(*The student studies in the afternoon.*)

Understanding these basic sentence structures will help you express simple ideas clearly in Japanese.

Exercises

Exercise 1: Vocabulary Review

Match the Japanese words to their English meanings:

1. 学生 → __
2. 病院 → __
3. 来る → __
4. 本 → __
5. 友達 → __
6. **すみません** → __
7. **お茶** → __
8. 駅 → __
9. 会う → __
10. 明日 → __

Options:

A. Book
B. Student
C. Train station
D. Hospital
E. To come
F. Tomorrow
G. Friend
H. Excuse me / I'm sorry
I. To meet
J. Tea

Exercise 2: Fill in the Sentence

Complete each sentence using the correct word in Hiragana, Katakana, or Kanji:

1. 私は________を読みます。 (*I read a book.*)

   ○ Options: 本, りんご, 車

2. 学生は________に行きます。 (*The student goes to school.*)

   ○ Options: 家, 学校, 病院

3. 彼女は________を食べます。 (*She eats an apple.*)

   ○ Options: 本, りんご, パン

4. 私は＿＿＿＿＿＿を飲みます。 (*I drink tea.*)

   ○ Options: お茶, コーヒー, パン

5. 友達は＿＿＿＿＿＿にいます。 (*My friend is in the library.*)

   ○ Options: 学校, 図書館, 銀行

Exercise 3: Sentence Translation

Translate the following sentences into Japanese using the correct vocabulary and particles:

1. I go to the bank.
2. He drinks coffee.
3. We eat bread.
4. The teacher reads a book.
5. You go to the supermarket.

Exercise 4: Mixed Sentence Practice

Choose the correct Kanji or Katakana to complete the sentences:

1. 私は＿＿＿＿＿＿を見ます。 (*I watch a movie.*)

   ○ Options: 映画, 先生, 友達

2. 月曜日に＿＿＿＿＿＿へ行きます。 (*I go to school on Monday.*)

   ○ Options: 病院, 学校, 喫茶店

3. 彼女は＿＿＿＿＿＿を聞きます。 (*She listens to music.*)

   ○ Options: りんご, 音楽, コーヒー

4. 私は＿＿＿＿＿＿を買います。 (*I buy a car.*)

   ○ Options: 本, 車, 家

5. 今日は＿＿＿＿＿＿ですか？ (*Is today Sunday?*)

   ○ Options: 土曜日, 月曜日, 日曜日

Answer Key

Exercise 1: Vocabulary Review

1. 学生 → B. Student
2. 病院 → D. Hospital
3. 来る → E. To come
4. 本 → A. Book
5. 友達 → G. Friend
6. すみません → H. Excuse me / I'm sorry
7. お茶 → J. Tea
8. 駅 → C. Train station
9. 会う → I. To meet
10. 明日 → F. Tomorrow

Exercise 2: Fill in the Sentence

1. 私は本を読みます。(*I read a book.*)
2. 学生は学校に行きます。(*The student goes to school.*)
3. 彼女はりんごを食べます。(*She eats an apple.*)
4. 私はお茶を飲みます。(*I drink tea.*)
5. 友達は図書館にいます。(*My friend is in the library.*)

Exercise 3: Sentence Translation

1. **I go to the bank**: 私は銀行に行きます。(*Watashi wa ginkou ni ikimasu.*)
2. **He drinks coffee**: 彼はコーヒーを飲みます。(*Kare wa ko-hi- o nomimasu.*)
3. **We eat bread**: 私たちはパンを食べます。(*Watashitachi wa pan o tabemasu.*)
4. **The teacher reads a book**: 先生は本を読みます。(*Sensei wa hon o yomimasu.*)
5. **You go to the supermarket**: あなたはスーパーへ行きます。(*Anata wa su-pa- e ikimasu.*)

Exercise 4: Mixed Sentence Practice

1. 私は映画を見ます。(*I watch a movie.*)
2. 月曜日に学校へ行きます。(*I go to school on Monday.*)
3. 彼女は音楽を聞きます。(*She listens to music.*)
4. 私は車を買います。(*I buy a car.*)
5. 今日は日曜日ですか？(*Is today Sunday?*)

Chapter 7: Pronunciation and Listening Skills

"To learn a language is to have one more window from which to look at the world."
– Chinese Proverb

As with any language, mastering **pronunciation** and developing **listening skills** are crucial for effective communication. Even if you know the grammar and vocabulary, speaking Japanese accurately and understanding spoken Japanese in real time can be challenging without focused practice. This chapter will guide you through the **key elements of Japanese pronunciation** and introduce practical exercises to help you build your **listening comprehension**.

Japanese pronunciation is often considered simpler than English, as it has fewer sounds and follows a more consistent pattern. However, there are specific rules and nuances—such as **pitch accent**, **long and short vowels**, and the **R sound**—that require careful attention.

In this chapter, we'll cover the fundamentals of **Japanese pronunciation**, from mastering individual sounds to combining them smoothly in sentences. We'll also introduce some basic **listening techniques** to help you improve your ability to comprehend spoken Japanese in different contexts.

Let's begin with some **tips for proper pronunciation**!

Tips for Proper Pronunciation

Pronunciation is one of the most critical aspects of learning Japanese. Japanese sounds are relatively simple compared to English, but the key is to focus on **consistency and clarity**.

In this section, we'll break down the basics of Japanese pronunciation, covering essential points like **vowel sounds**, **consonant combinations**, and **pitch accents**.

Mastering these will ensure your spoken Japanese is clear and easily understood by native speakers.

1. Mastering the Japanese Vowel Sounds

Japanese has **five basic vowel sounds**, which are always pronounced the same way regardless of where they appear in a word. Each vowel should be **short, clear, and crisp**. Here's a breakdown:

Vowel	Romaji	Pronunciation Guide	Example
あ	*a*	Like the "ah" sound in *car*	あか (*aka* - red)
い	*i*	Like the "ee" sound in *see*	いぬ (*inu* - dog)
う	*u*	Like the "oo" sound in *food*	うみ (*umi* - sea)

| え | e | Like the "e" sound in *met* | えき (*eki* - station) |
| お | o | Like the "o" sound in *go* | おちゃ (*ocha* - tea) |

Tips:

- Keep vowel sounds **short** and avoid the English tendency to diphthongize (turning a vowel into two sounds, e.g., "a" in *say*).
- Practice saying each vowel repeatedly, ensuring that the sound remains **pure** and unchanged.

2. Long and Short Vowels

Japanese distinguishes between **short** and **long vowels**. Long vowels are held for **twice as long** as short vowels, which can change the meaning of a word entirely:

Short Vowel	Long Vowel	Example	Meaning
おじさん	おじいさん	*ojisan*	Uncle
		ojiisan	Grandfather
ここ	こうこう	*koko*	Here
		koukou	High school

Tips:

- Pay attention to **word length** when listening or speaking. Holding a vowel for just a fraction too long (or too short) can cause confusion.

3. Consonants and Combinations

Most Japanese consonants sound similar to their English counterparts, but there are a few that require special attention:

Consonant	Sound Characteristics	Example
R	The Japanese "R" sound is pronounced by lightly tapping the tongue against the roof of the mouth, like a blend of "L" and "D".	ら (ra), り (ri), る (ru), れ (re), ろ (ro)
S	The "S" sound is straightforward, except in し (*shi*), which is pronounced like the "sh" in *she*.	し (*shi*)
F	The "F" sound in Japanese, as in ふ (*fu*), is softer and produced by blowing air between the lips.	ふ (*fu*)

Tips:

- Practice each consonant sound by itself and then combine it with different vowels to see how the sound changes (e.g., *ra, ri, ru*).

4. Pronouncing the Small "っ" (Sokuon)

The small "っ" symbol (called *sokuon*) is used to indicate a **doubled consonant**. It creates a **pause** or **stop** in the word, which affects the rhythm and pronunciation:

Japanese	Romaji	Meaning
きって	*kitte*	Stamp
さっか	*sakka*	Writer
がっこう	*gakkou*	School

Tips:

- When you see a small "っ" in a word, add a **slight pause** before the consonant that follows. For example, in さっか (*sakka*), pause briefly before the "k" sound.

5. The Pitch Accent

Unlike English, which uses **stress accents** (emphasizing certain syllables), Japanese uses a **pitch accent**. The pitch accent can change the meaning of words that otherwise sound the same:

Word	Romaji	Pitch Pattern	Meaning
はし	*hashi*	High-Low	Chopsticks
はし	*hashi*	Low-High	Bridge
あめ	*ame*	Low-High	Candy
あめ	*ame*	High-Low	Rain

Tips:

- To master pitch accent, start by listening carefully to native speakers and mimic their pronunciation patterns.
- Use online tools or resources with pitch accent markings to practice.

Key Takeaways

❖ **Japanese pronunciation** follows a consistent pattern, with clear, short vowels and straightforward consonants.

❖ Pay close attention to the distinction between **long and short vowels**—incorrect vowel length can completely change the meaning of a word.

❖ Practice the unique Japanese **"R" sound** by tapping the tongue lightly against the roof of your mouth, and learn the usage of **small "っ" (sokuon)** to indicate a doubled consonant sound.

❖ Japanese uses a **pitch accent** rather than a stress accent. This means that pitch (high or low) differentiates words with similar syllables.

❖ **Listening comprehension** requires more than just vocabulary knowledge. Focus on picking out **keywords**, using **context clues**, and understanding basic sentence structures.

❖ Gradually increase the **speed and complexity** of listening materials to build your skills step-by-step.

❖ Use **shadowing**, **repetition**, and **context-based listening** to reinforce your understanding and improve both your pronunciation and listening skills.

Exercises

Exercise 1: Pronunciation Practice

Read the following Japanese words aloud, paying attention to the correct pronunciation of vowels and consonants. Write down their meanings if you know them:

1. あめ (*ame*)
2. おばあさん (*obaasan*)
3. はし (*hashi*)
4. さっか (*sakka*)
5. がっこう (*gakkou*)
6. おちゃ (*ocha*)
7. こうこう (*koukou*)
8. ふじさん (*Fujisan*)
9. かんじ (*kanji*)
10. しゃしん (*shashin*)

Exercise 2: Pitch Accent Identification

For each pair of words below, identify the **pitch accent** (High-Low or Low-High). Write down the English meaning of each word:

1. はし (*hashi*)
   - Option 1: High-Low – Chopsticks
   - Option 2: Low-High – Bridge

2. あめ (*ame*)
   - Option 1: High-Low – Rain
   - Option 2: Low-High – Candy

3. いま (*ima*)
   - Option 1: High-Low – Living room
   - Option 2: Low-High – Now

4. さけ (*sake*)
   - Option 1: High-Low – Alcohol
   - Option 2: Low-High – Salmon

5. かみ (*kami*)
   - Option 1: High-Low – Hair
   - Option 2: Low-High – Paper

Exercise 3: Listening Comprehension Practice
Read the following sentence aloud and identify the **keywords** in the sentence. Then, write down the general meaning:

Sentence:
"私は月曜日に図書館で本を読みます。"
(*Watashi wa getsuyoubi ni toshokan de hon o yomimasu.*)

Keywords to focus on:

- Subject: 私 (*watashi*)

- Time: 月曜日 (*getsuyoubi*)

- Place: 図書館 (*toshokan*)

- Object: 本 (*hon*)

- Verb: 読みます (*yomimasu*)

Question:
What is the speaker doing, where, and on what day?

Exercise 4: Shadowing Practice
Choose a short Japanese sentence from below, listen to it (or read it aloud yourself), and then **repeat** the sentence while mimicking the **pitch, rhythm, and intonation** as closely as possible:

1. 私はすしを食べます。
   - *Watashi wa sushi o tabemasu.*
   - Meaning: I eat sushi.

2. 彼は日本に行きます。
   - *Kare wa Nihon ni ikimasu.*
   - Meaning: He goes to Japan.

3. お茶を飲みますか？
   - *Ocha o nomimasu ka?*
   - Meaning: Do you drink tea?

4. 私はテレビを見ます。
   - *Watashi wa terebi o mimasu.*
   - Meaning: I watch TV.

Tips:

- Listen to each sentence multiple times until you're familiar with the sound pattern.
- Focus on reproducing the **natural flow** of the sentence rather than individual sounds.

Answer Key

Exercise 1: Pronunciation Practice

1. あめ (*ame*) – Candy / Rain
2. おばあさん (*obaasan*) – Grandmother
3. はし (*hashi*) – Chopsticks / Bridge
4. さっか (*sakka*) – Writer
5. がっこう (*gakkou*) – School
6. おちゃ (*ocha*) – Tea
7. こうこう (*koukou*) – High school
8. ふじさん (*Fujisan*) – Mt. Fuji
9. かんじ (*kanji*) – Kanji (Chinese characters)
10. しゃしん (*shashin*) – Photograph

Exercise 2: Pitch Accent Identification

1. はし:
    - **Option 1 (High-Low)** – Chopsticks
    - **Option 2 (Low-High)** – Bridge
2. あめ:
    - **Option 1 (High-Low)** – Rain
    - **Option 2 (Low-High)** – Candy
3. いま:
    - **Option 1 (High-Low)** – Living room
    - **Option 2 (Low-High)** – Now
4. さけ:
    - **Option 1 (High-Low)** – Alcohol
    - **Option 2 (Low-High)** – Salmon
5. かみ:
    - **Option 1 (High-Low)** – Hair
    - **Option 2 (Low-High)** – Paper

Exercise 3: Listening Comprehension Practice
"私は月曜日に図書館で本を読みます。"
(*Watashi wa getsuyoubi ni toshokan de hon o yomimasu.*)
Answer:
The speaker reads a book at the library on Monday.

Exercise 4: Shadowing Practice
Try repeating each sentence until you feel comfortable with the flow and pronunciation!

Conclusion

Congratulations on completing this guide! Throughout this book, you've laid a solid foundation in the Japanese language, mastering essential vocabulary, grammar structures, and pronunciation skills. From learning the basics of Hiragana and Katakana to understanding the complexities of Kanji, you've built up the tools needed to start reading, writing, and speaking Japanese with confidence.

But remember, this is only the beginning of your journey. Learning a language is a lifelong process that requires consistent practice and real-world application. Take what you've learned and put it into action by engaging in conversations, practicing with native speakers, exploring Japanese media, or even planning a trip to Japan. The more you use your Japanese in authentic settings, the stronger your language skills will become.

As we conclude for now, keep pushing forward. Revisit key concepts, continue expanding your vocabulary, and challenge yourself to use Japanese in new and meaningful ways. The path to fluency is not always easy, but you'll continue to see progress with dedication and persistence.

頑張って (Ganbatte) and keep moving forward! I look forward to seeing you continue your journey to mastering Japanese. またね (Matane)—see you soon!

BOOK 2

The Essential Japanese Workbook for Beginners:

Practice Hiragana, Katakana, and Kanji With Step-by-Step Exercises

Explore to Win

Book Description

Are you looking for a structured, comprehensive way to solidify your Japanese language skills? Do you want to practice what you've learned and build your confidence in reading, writing, and speaking? Whether you're a complete beginner or someone who wants to revisit the basics, **"The Essential Japanese Workbook for Beginners"** is designed just for you!

This workbook is a step-by-step guide to help you master **Hiragana**, **Katakana**, and **Kanji** through targeted exercises, vocabulary building, and sentence construction practice. Each chapter is filled with activities reinforcing your understanding and providing hands-on learning experiences, ensuring you can apply what you've learned in real-world scenarios.

Inside this essential workbook, you'll find:

- **Core vocabulary lists** covering **nouns, verbs, and adjectives** to build a strong foundation
- **Reading and writing drills** for **Hiragana, Katakana, and basic Kanji**, along with flashcards for quick review
- **Grammar exercises** that introduce key concepts, such as verb conjugation and sentence structure, making Japanese grammar accessible and easy to follow
- **Thematic vocabulary and dialogues**, such as phrases for shopping, dining, and giving directions, so you can navigate everyday situations with ease
- **Practical conversation practice**, where you'll apply what you've learned to common interactions, from introducing yourself to making small talk

This workbook is more than just a collection of exercises—it's your guide to putting Japanese into practice, step by step. By the end of this book, you'll be able to read and write basic Japanese sentences, understand essential grammar structures, and communicate confidently in various settings.

Ready to take your Japanese skills to the next level? Let's begin your journey to mastering the basics with **"The Essential Japanese Workbook for Beginners"**!

Introduction

Welcome to *The Essential Japanese Workbook for Beginners*! This workbook is designed to be your hands-on companion as you develop your Japanese reading, writing, and speaking skills. Whether you've just started learning Japanese or want to reinforce what you already know, this book will provide you with the tools and exercises to turn theoretical knowledge into practical use.

Throughout this workbook, you'll find a variety of **exercises**, **vocabulary drills**, and **sentence-building activities** that cover the fundamentals of Japanese. Each chapter focuses on a specific aspect of the language—from **vocabulary building** and **grammar practice** to constructing complete sentences and engaging in **simple conversations**. We'll guide you through the learning process step-by-step, making it easy to build up your skills incrementally.

Our approach is straightforward: you'll learn by **doing**. The workbook format is meant to be interactive, with plenty of opportunities for **hands-on practice**. You'll start by mastering the basics of Hiragana and Katakana, then move on to reading and writing simple Kanji. As you progress, you'll expand your vocabulary, practice forming sentences, and eventually apply these skills in real-world conversations.

By completing this workbook, you'll solidify your understanding of the Japanese writing system and gain the confidence to use it in daily life. Whether you aim to improve your Japanese for travel, work, or personal enjoyment, this book will help you achieve your goals.

Let's dive in and get ready to turn your knowledge into practice!

Chapter 1: Building a Strong Vocabulary Foundation

"A different language is a different vision of life."
– Federico Fellini

Before diving into complex grammar structures or practicing conversations, building a **solid vocabulary foundation** is essential. In this chapter, you'll focus on learning and practicing the most commonly used **nouns**, **verbs**, and **adjectives**. Having a broad vocabulary set is crucial for expressing yourself clearly and understanding basic Japanese texts and dialogues.

We'll start with a selection of **essential words** for describing people, places, and everyday objects. Then, we'll move on to common **verbs** used in daily actions and practical contexts, followed by a set of **adjectives** that will help you describe the world around you. This core vocabulary will serve as the building blocks for constructing sentences and engaging in simple conversations as you progress through the workbook.

By the end of this chapter, you'll have a strong vocabulary base, allowing you to confidently name people, places, and things, as well as perform basic actions using the verbs and adjectives you've learned.

Let's get started by building your vocabulary with some **essential nouns**!

Essential Nouns, Verbs, and Adjectives

Let's begin by breaking down the three main categories of vocabulary—**nouns**, **verbs**, and **adjectives**—that you'll use frequently in daily Japanese communication.

1. Essential Nouns

Nouns are the backbone of every language, allowing you to name people, places, and things. Below, you'll find key nouns grouped into useful categories. For each noun, I'll provide the **Kanji or Kana**, the **Romaji**, and the **English meaning**.

People

Japanese	Romaji	Meaning
私	*watashi*	I / Me
あなた	*anata*	You
彼	*kare*	He / Him

彼女	*kanojo*	She / Her
友達	*tomodachi*	Friend
学生	*gakusei*	Student
先生	*sensei*	Teacher
母	*haha*	Mother
父	*chichi*	Father

Places

Japanese	Romaji	Meaning
学校	*gakkou*	School
図書館	*toshokan*	Library
銀行	*ginkou*	Bank
公園	*kouen*	Park
病院	*byouin*	Hospital
家	*ie*	House / Home
郵便局	*yuubinkyoku*	Post office
駅	*eki*	Train station
スーパー	*su-pa-*	Supermarket

Things

Japanese	Romaji	Meaning
本	*hon*	Book
机	*tsukue*	Desk
車	*kuruma*	Car
いす	*isu*	Chair
テレビ	*terebi*	TV
コンピュータ	*konpyu-ta*	Computer
時計	*tokei*	Clock / Watch
ドア	*doa*	Door
鞄	*kaban*	Bag

2. Common Verbs

Verbs allow you to describe **actions**. Here are some of the most commonly used Japanese verbs that will help you express what you or others are doing. Each verb is listed in its **dictionary form**, which is the most basic form of the verb.

Japanese	Romaji	Meaning
行く	*iku*	To go
来る	*kuru*	To come
見る	*miru*	To see / To watch
食べる	*taberu*	To eat

飲む	*nomu*	To drink
読む	*yomu*	To read
書く	*kaku*	To write
会う	*au*	To meet
話す	*hanasu*	To speak
聞く	*kiku*	To listen / To ask
買う	*kau*	To buy
する	*suru*	To do
勉強する	*benkyou suru*	To study

Note: Many verbs, like *benkyou suru* (to study), are combinations of a noun (勉強, meaning "study") and the verb する (*suru*, meaning "to do"). This pattern is common in Japanese and will be introduced more thoroughly in later chapters.

3. Essential Adjectives

Adjectives in Japanese are used to describe **qualities** or **states** of people and objects. They are divided into two main categories: **い-adjectives** and **な-adjectives**, depending on their endings.

い-Adjectives

Japanese	Romaji	Meaning
大きい	*ookii*	Big
小さい	*chiisai*	Small
新しい	*atarashii*	New
古い	*furui*	Old

いい	*ii*	Good
悪い	*warui*	Bad
高い	*takai*	Tall / Expensive
安い	*yasui*	Cheap
美しい	*utsukushii*	Beautiful

な-Adjectives

Japanese	**Romaji**	**Meaning**
きれいな	*kireina*	Clean / Pretty
元気な	*genkina*	Energetic / Healthy
静かな	*shizukana*	Quiet
有名な	*yuumeina*	Famous
親切な	*shinsetsuna*	Kind
簡単な	*kantanna*	Simple / Easy

Next, we'll see how to use these nouns, verbs, and adjectives in context through sentence-building exercises. Let's move on to **Vocabulary for People, Places, and Things**, where you'll practice using your new words to describe common scenarios.

Vocabulary for People, Places, and Things

Now that you have a collection of essential nouns, verbs, and adjectives, let's dive deeper into using them to talk about **people**, **places**, and **things** in everyday contexts.

Describing and identifying people, navigating different locations, and talking about objects in your environment are critical language skills that will help you in real-world situations.

1. Describing People

Use the following patterns and vocabulary to describe yourself and others:

1. **Describing Yourself (I am a…)**
   私は学生です。(*Watashi wa gakusei desu.*) – I am a student.
   彼は先生です。(*Kare wa sensei desu.*) – He is a teacher.

2. **Talking About Family Members**
   母は親切です。(*Haha wa shinsetsu desu.*) – My mother is kind.
   父は元気です。(*Chichi wa genki desu.*) – My father is energetic.

3. **Using Adjectives to Describe People**
   彼女はきれいです。(*Kanojo wa kirei desu.*) – She is pretty.
   私の友達は静かです。(*Watashi no tomodachi wa shizuka desu.*) – My friend is quiet.

Practice: Try describing people in your life using the patterns above. What words can you use to describe your family members or friends?

2. Talking About Places

Use location-related vocabulary to describe where you or someone else is going or located.

1. **Basic Sentence Pattern: Subject は Place に います / 行きます**

   - 学生は学校にいます。(*Gakusei wa gakkou ni imasu.*) – The student is at school.

   - 私は図書館に行きます。(*Watashi wa toshokan ni ikimasu.*) – I go to the library.

2. **Using Nouns and Verbs Together**

   - 銀行でお金を引き出します。(*Ginkou de okane o hikidashimasu.*) – I withdraw money at the bank.

   - 公園で遊びます。(*Kouen de asobimasu.*) – I play at the park.

Practice: Write a few sentences about where you usually go during the day. For example: "I go to the supermarket," or "My friend is at the hospital."

3. Describing Objects and Things

Use adjectives and verbs to describe everyday items and objects.

1. **Basic Sentence Pattern: Object は Adjective です。**

   - 本は面白いです。(*Hon wa omoshiroi desu.*) – The book is interesting.

   - 車は高いです。(*Kuruma wa takai desu.*) – The car is expensive.

2. **Using Adjectives to Compare**

   - 私の鞄は小さいです。(*Watashi no kaban wa chiisai desu.*) – My bag is small.

   - テレビは新しいです。(*Terebi wa atarashii desu.*) – The TV is new.

3. **Talking About Possession: Using の (no)**
   - これは私の本です。(*Kore wa watashi no hon desu.*) – This is my book.
   - あなたの時計はどこですか？(*Anata no tokei wa doko desu ka?*) – Where is your watch?

Practice: Look around the room you're in and try describing three objects using the sentence patterns above.

Example Sentences

To help reinforce your understanding, here are some example sentences using people, places, and things:

1. **People**:
   - 友達は先生です。(*Tomodachi wa sensei desu.*) – My friend is a teacher.
   - 彼はとても親切な人です。(*Kare wa totemo shinsetsuna hito desu.*) – He is a very kind person.
2. **Places**:
   - 図書館は静かです。(*Toshokan wa shizuka desu.*) – The library is quiet.
   - 駅はどこですか？(*Eki wa doko desu ka?*) – Where is the train station?
3. **Things**:
   - この鞄は高いです。(*Kono kaban wa takai desu.*) – This bag is expensive.
   - その本は面白いですか？(*Sono hon wa omoshiroi desu ka?*) – Is that book interesting?

Key Takeaways

- ❖ Use **nouns** to name people, places, and things in your environment.
- ❖ Practice basic sentence patterns to describe **people** (e.g., 私は学生です - I am a student) and their qualities using adjectives (e.g., 彼女はきれいです - She is pretty).
- ❖ Use **location words** to talk about where people or things are.
- ❖ Describe **objects** using basic adjectives and **possessive constructions** (e.g., 私の本 - My book).
- ❖ Understanding these basic vocabulary and sentence patterns will enable you to engage in simple conversations and descriptions.

Exercises

Exercise 1: Vocabulary Matching

Match the Japanese words to their English meanings:

1. 私 → ___
2. 学校 → ___
3. 車 → ___
4. 大きい → ___
5. 先生 → ___
6. 飲む → ___
7. 銀行 → ___
8. きれいな → ___

Options:

A. To drink
B. Teacher
C. Big
D. I / Me
E. Bank
F. Car
G. School
H. Clean / Pretty

Exercise 2: Fill in the Blanks

Complete the following sentences with the correct vocabulary word from the chapter:

1. 私は____です。(I am ___.)
   Options: 学生, 先生

2. 彼女は____です。(She is ___.)
   Options: きれい, 悪い

3. 学校は____です。(The school is ___.)
   Options: 静か, 高い

4. 銀行に____を引き出します。(I withdraw ____ at the bank.)
   Options: 車, お金

5. 私の____は小さいです。(My ____ is small.)
   Options: 鞄, 本

Exercise 3: Translate the Sentences

Translate the following sentences into Japanese:

1. I am a student.
2. The library is quiet.
3. He is a kind person.
4. This car is expensive.
5. Where is your bag?

Exercise 4: Sentence Creation

Using the vocabulary from the chapter, create sentences based on the following prompts:

1. Describe yourself using an adjective.
2. Talk about where you usually go during the day.
3. Describe an object in your room.
4. Ask someone about their hobbies using a verb.

Answer Key

Answer to Exercise 1: Vocabulary Matching

1. 私 → D. I / Me
2. 学校 → G. School
3. 車 → F. Car
4. 大きい → C. Big
5. 先生 → B. Teacher
6. 飲む → A. To drink
7. 銀行 → E. Bank
8. きれいな → H. Clean / Pretty

Answer to Exercise 2: Fill in the Blanks

1. 私は**学生**です。(I am a student.)
2. 彼女は**きれい**です。(She is pretty.)
3. 学校は**静か**です。(The school is quiet.)
4. 銀行に**お金**を引き出します。(I withdraw money at the bank.)
5. 私の**鞄**は小さいです。(My bag is small.)

Answer to Exercise 3: Translate the Sentences

1. 私は学生です。(Watashi wa gakusei desu.)
2. 図書館は静かです。(Toshokan wa shizuka desu.)
3. 彼は親切な人です。(Kare wa shinsetsuna hito desu.)
4. この車は高いです。(Kono kuruma wa takai desu.)
5. あなたの鞄はどこですか？(Anata no kaban wa doko desu ka?)

Answer to Exercise 4: Sentence Creation

(Example Responses)

1. 私は学生です。(Watashi wa gakusei desu.) – I am a student.
2. 私は学校に行きます。(Watashi wa gakkou ni ikimasu.) – I go to school.
3. この本は面白いです。(Kono hon wa omoshiroi desu.) – This book is interesting.
4. あなたの趣味は何ですか？(Anata no shumi wa nan desu ka?) – What are your hobbies?

Chapter 2: Constructing Basic Sentences

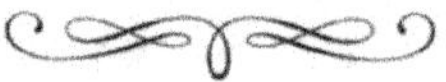

"Language shapes the way we think, and determines what we can think about."
– Benjamin Lee Whorf

Now that you've built a solid foundation of essential vocabulary, it's time to start constructing **basic sentences**. This chapter will introduce you to the fundamental elements of Japanese sentence structure and show you how to put together words to express your thoughts clearly.

Japanese sentence construction may seem complex at first, but it follows a consistent pattern that becomes easier with practice. The key difference between Japanese and English is the **order of elements** in a sentence. Mastering the Japanese sentence structure is essential for forming clear and grammatically correct sentences.

By the end of this chapter, you'll be able to create your own basic sentences, ask simple questions, and describe everyday actions confidently. Let's start by breaking down the **core components** of a Japanese sentence!

Understanding Sentence Structure

In English, we use **Subject-Verb-Object (SVO)**, while in Japanese, we use **Subject-Object-Verb (SOV)**. This means that the verb always appears **at the end** of a Japanese sentence. This may feel unfamiliar at first, but it becomes easier with practice.

Let's break down the basic components of a Japanese sentence and how they fit together:

1. Basic Sentence Structure: Subject-Object-Verb (SOV)

The simplest Japanese sentence pattern is:
[Subject] + [Object] + [Verb]

- **Subject**: The person or thing performing the action
- **Object**: The target or receiver of the action
- **Verb**: The action itself, which always appears at the **end** of the sentence

Example:

- 私はりんごを食べます。
  Watashi wa ringo o tabemasu.
  Meaning: I eat an apple.
    - Subject: 私 (*watashi*) – I
    - Object: りんご (*ringo*) – Apple
    - Verb: 食べます (*tabemasu*) – To eat

Notice that unlike in English, where the verb appears between the subject and the object ("I eat an apple"), Japanese places the verb at the **end** of the sentence.

2. Using Particles to Define Sentence Roles

In Japanese, **particles** are small words that follow nouns and indicate their grammatical role in the sentence. Think of them as **markers** that tell us what each word is doing in the sentence. Here are some of the most common particles and their functions:

Particle	Pronunciation	Usage	Example Sentence
は	*wa*	Marks the **subject** or **topic**	私は学生です。(*Watashi wa gakusei desu.*) – I am a student.
を	*wo* (pronounced as "o")	Marks the **direct object** of a verb	本を読みます。(*Hon o yomimasu.*) – I read a book.
に	*ni*	Indicates **destination** or **point in time**	学校に行きます。(*Gakkou ni ikimasu.*) – I go to school.
で	*de*	Indicates **location** or **means**	図書館で勉強します。(*Toshokan de benkyou shimasu.*) – I study at the library.

Key Points:

- は (*wa*) introduces the **subject** or **topic** of the sentence.
- を (*wo*) identifies the **direct object**—what is being acted upon.
- に (*ni*) often marks a **destination** or **specific time** (e.g., "to the park" or "at 3 o'clock").
- で (*de*) marks the **place of action** or the **means** by which an action is performed (e.g., "at the library" or "by train").

3. Putting It All Together: Building Simple Sentences

Now, let's see how to put these elements together to form sentences. We'll start with a few examples:

- 私は本を読みます。
  Watashi wa hon o yomimasu.
  Meaning: I read a book.
  - Subject: 私 (*watashi*) – I

- Object: 本 (*hon*) – Book
- Verb: 読みます (*yomimasu*) – To read

- 彼は学校に行きます。
  Kare wa gakkou ni ikimasu.
  Meaning: He goes to school.
    - Subject: 彼 (*kare*) – He
    - Object: 学校 (*gakkou*) – School
    - Verb: 行きます (*ikimasu*) – To go

4. Expanding the Sentence: Adding Time and Place

You can add more detail to your sentences by specifying **time** and **place** using particles:

- 私は月曜日に図書館で勉強します。
  Watashi wa getsuyoubi ni toshokan de benkyou shimasu.
  Meaning: I study at the library on Monday.
    - Subject: 私 (*watashi*) – I
    - Time: 月曜日に (*getsuyoubi ni*) – On Monday
    - Place: 図書館で (*toshokan de*) – At the library
    - Verb: 勉強します (*benkyou shimasu*) – To study

5. Asking Questions: Using the Particle か (ka)

To turn a statement into a **question**, simply add the particle **か (ka)** at the end of the sentence:

- あなたは学生ですか？
  Anata wa gakusei desu ka?
  Meaning: Are you a student?
    - Add か (*ka*) to the end of 私は学生です (*watashi wa gakusei desu*) to create a question.

- これはりんごですか？
  Kore wa ringo desu ka?
  Meaning: Is this an apple?

Practice Sentences

Let's see if you can put together some sentences using what you've learned so far:

1. **I drink water** → 私は________を飲みます。
2. **She goes to the park** → 彼女は________に行きます。
3. **The student reads a book at the library** → 学生は________で本を読みます。

4. **Are you a teacher?** → あなたは________ですか？

Take a moment to try forming these sentences, and then we'll practice using more particles and sentence variations in the next section.

Using Particles in Context

Particles are a fundamental part of Japanese grammar, functioning as **markers** that define the relationship between words in a sentence. Using particles correctly is essential for constructing clear and meaningful sentences.

In this section, we'll explore the key particles in more depth and practice using them in a variety of contexts to build more complex sentences.

1. Common Particles and Their Functions

Here's a quick reference guide for some of the most frequently used Japanese particles:

Particle	Usage	Explanation	Example
は (*wa*)	Marks the **subject** or **topic**	Indicates the topic of the sentence—often the subject, but not always	私は学生です。 (*Watashi wa gakusei desu.*) – I am a student.
を (*wo*)	Marks the **direct object**	Used for the object that the action is performed on	本を読みます。 (*Hon o yomimasu.*) – I read a book.
に (*ni*)	Marks a **location**, **destination**, or **time**	Used to indicate the destination, place of existence, or specific time	図書館に行きます。 (*Toshokan ni ikimasu.*) – I go to the library.
で (*de*)	Indicates the **place of action** or **means**	Used for the location where an action occurs or to express how an action is performed (e.g., by train)	学校で勉強します。 (*Gakkou de benkyou shimasu.*) – I study at school.
の (*no*)	Shows **possession** or **modification**	Connects nouns, indicating ownership or describing one noun with another	私の本です。 (*Watashi no hon desu.*) – It is my book.

へ (e)	Marks **direction** or **destination**	Similar to に (ni), but focuses more on the direction rather than the endpoint	家へ帰ります。(*Ie e kaerimasu.*) – I go home.

2. Using Particles in Different Contexts

Let's see how to apply these particles in various sentence patterns to convey different types of information.

A. Describing Location and Destination with に (*ni*) and で (*de*)

- に (*ni*) is used to indicate a **location** where someone or something **exists** or a **destination** to which someone **moves**.
    - Example:
      学校にいます。(*Gakkou ni imasu.*) – I am at school.
      図書館に行きます。(*Toshokan ni ikimasu.*) – I go to the library.
- で (*de*) is used to show where an **action** is **performed**.
    - Example:
      学校で勉強します。(*Gakkou de benkyou shimasu.*) – I study at school.
      レストランで食べます。(*Resutoran de tabemasu.*) – I eat at the restaurant.

Practice: Try to create sentences using に and で, specifying locations where actions happen and where people are going.

B. Indicating the Object of an Action with を (*wo*)

を is used to mark the **object** of an action (e.g., what is being eaten, read, or seen).

- Example:
  本を読みます。(*Hon o yomimasu.*) – I read a book.
  りんごを食べます。(*Ringo o tabemasu.*) – I eat an apple.
  テレビを見ます。(*Terebi o mimasu.*) – I watch TV.

Practice: Choose an object and combine it with a verb you've learned to create sentences using を.

C. Expressing Possession or Relationship with の (*no*)

の is used to show **possession** or **modification**, connecting two nouns.

- Example:
  私の車です。(*Watashi no kuruma desu.*) – It is my car.
  先生の本です。(*Sensei no hon desu.*) – It is the teacher's book.

- It can also be used to describe one noun with another:
  日本の食べ物。(*Nihon no tabemono.*) – Japanese food.

Practice: Try using *の* to express ownership or describe something using two nouns.

3. Complex Sentences: Combining Particles

Once you're comfortable using individual particles, you can start combining them to create more complex sentences. Let's look at a few examples:

- 私は月曜日に学校で勉強します。
  Watashi wa getsuyoubi ni gakkou de benkyou shimasu.
  Meaning: I study at school on Monday.
    - は (*wa*): Topic marker ("I")
    - に (*ni*): Time marker ("on Monday")
    - で (*de*): Location marker ("at school")

- 彼女は午後に図書館で本を読みます。
  Kanojo wa gogo ni toshokan de hon o yomimasu.
  Meaning: She reads a book at the library in the afternoon.
    - は (*wa*): Topic marker ("She")
    - に (*ni*): Time marker ("in the afternoon")
    - で (*de*): Location marker ("at the library")
    - を (*wo*): Object marker ("book")

Practice: Create your own sentences by combining different particles and vocabulary.

Key Takeaways

- ❖ **Japanese sentence structure** follows the **Subject-Object-Verb (SOV)** pattern, meaning that the verb always appears at the end of the sentence.

- ❖ **Particles** are essential in Japanese for defining the **roles** of words in a sentence. Some of the key particles to remember are:
    - ➢ は (***wa***): Marks the **topic** or **subject** of the sentence
    - ➢ を (***wo***): Indicates the **direct object** of a verb
    - ➢ に (***ni***): Used for indicating **destination**, **specific time**, or **indirect objects**
    - ➢ で (***de***): Used for indicating **location** or **means** by which an action is performed

- ❖ When building sentences, use particles to **link** words together and clarify the **relationships** between the **subject**, **object**, and **action**.

- ❖ To form **questions**, add the particle か (***ka***) at the end of a statement.

Exercises

Exercise 1: Complete the Sentences Using Particles
Fill in the blanks with the correct particles (は, を, に, or で):

1. 私＿＿＿学校＿＿＿行きます。 (*Watashi ＿＿＿ gakkou ＿＿＿ ikimasu.*) – I go to school.
2. 図書館＿＿＿本＿＿＿読みます。 (*Toshokan ＿＿＿ hon ＿＿＿ yomimasu.*) – I read a book at the library.
3. 彼＿＿＿月曜日＿＿＿来ます。 (*Kare ＿＿＿ getsuyoubi ＿＿＿ kimasu.*) – He comes on Monday.
4. 公園＿＿＿友達＿＿＿会います。 (*Kouen ＿＿＿ tomodachi ＿＿＿ aimasu.*) – I meet my friend at the park.
5. あなた＿＿＿お茶＿＿＿飲みますか？ (*Anata ＿＿＿ ocha ＿＿＿ nomimasu ka?*) – Do you drink tea?

Options: は, を, に, で

Exercise 2: Translate the Sentence into Japanese
Use the correct particles to translate the following sentences:

1. I eat sushi at the restaurant.
2. She buys a book at the bookstore.
3. We study at the library on Tuesday.
4. Do you watch TV at home?
5. He meets his friend at 5 o'clock.

Exercise 3: Identify the Particle and Its Function
Read the following sentences and identify the particle used and its function (e.g., は: Topic marker, を: Direct object, etc.):

1. 私は映画を見ます。 (*Watashi wa eiga o mimasu.*)
   - **Particle**: ＿＿＿ – Function: ＿＿＿
2. 先生は学生に話します。 (*Sensei wa gakusei ni hanashimasu.*)
   - **Particle**: ＿＿＿ – Function: ＿＿＿
3. 家でテレビを見ます。 (*Ie de terebi o mimasu.*)
   - **Particle**: ＿＿＿ – Function: ＿＿＿
4. 友達に本をあげます。 (*Tomodachi ni hon o agemasu.*)
   - **Particle**: ＿＿＿ – Function: ＿＿＿
5. 公園で走ります。 (*Kouen de hashirimasu.*)

Exercise 4: Question Formation Practice

Turn the following sentences into questions by adding the particle **か** *(ka)*:

1. あなたは学生です。 (*Anata wa gakusei desu.*) – You are a student.

2. 彼は日本に行きます。 (*Kare wa Nihon ni ikimasu.*) – He goes to Japan.

3. 彼女はお茶を飲みます。 (*Kanojo wa ocha o nomimasu.*) – She drinks tea.

4. 私はテレビを見ます。 (*Watashi wa terebi o mimasu.*) – I watch TV.

5. あなたは学校にいます。 (*Anata wa gakkou ni imasu.*) – You are at school.

Answer Key

Exercise 1: Complete the Sentences Using Particles

1. 私**は**学校**に**行きます。(*Watashi **wa** gakkou **ni** ikimasu.*) – I go to school.
2. 図書館**で**本**を**読みます。(*Toshokan **de** hon **o** yomimasu.*) – I read a book at the library.
3. 彼**は**月曜日**に**来ます。(*Kare **wa** getsuyoubi **ni** kimasu.*) – He comes on Monday.
4. 公園**で**友達**に**会います。(*Kouen **de** tomodachi **ni** aimasu.*) – I meet my friend at the park.
5. あなたはお茶を飲みますか？(*Anata **wa** ocha **o** nomimasu ka?*) – Do you drink tea?

Exercise 2: Translate the Sentence into Japanese

1. 私はレストランで寿司を食べます。(*Watashi wa resutoran de sushi o tabemasu.*)
2. 彼女は本屋で本を買います。(*Kanojo wa honya de hon o kaimasu.*)
3. 私たちは火曜日に図書館で勉強します。(*Watashitachi wa kayoubi ni toshokan de benkyou shimasu.*)
4. あなたは家でテレビを見ますか？(*Anata wa ie de terebi o mimasu ka?*)
5. 彼は5時に友達に会います。(*Kare wa goji ni tomodachi ni aimasu.*)

Exercise 3: Identify the Particle and Its Function

1. **を**: Direct object marker
2. **に**: Indirect object (receiver)
3. **で**: Location of action
4. **に**: Indirect object (to someone)
5. **で**: Location of action

Exercise 4: Question Formation Practice

1. あなたは学生ですか？ (*Anata wa gakusei desu ka?*)
2. 彼は日本に行きますか？ (*Kare wa Nihon ni ikimasu ka?*)
3. 彼女はお茶を飲みますか？ (*Kanojo wa ocha o nomimasu ka?*)
4. 私はテレビを見ますか？ (*Watashi wa terebi o mimasu ka?*)
5. あなたは学校にいますか？ (*Anata wa gakkou ni imasu ka?*)

Chapter 3: The Basics of Japanese Grammar

"Language is the dress of thought."
– Samuel Johnson

Now that you have a grasp of basic sentence structure and particles, it's time to delve into **Japanese grammar**—specifically, how verbs work. Verbs are the **action words** that drive a sentence, and understanding their conjugation patterns will enable you to accurately express different actions and states.

In Japanese, verbs are **conjugated** to show **tense** (past, present, future), **negation**, and **politeness**. This means that the **ending** of a verb changes depending on the context. Fortunately, Japanese verb conjugation is systematic and follows a predictable pattern once you understand the basic rules.

This chapter will introduce you to:

1. **Verb Conjugation Basics**: Learn the main verb groups and how to conjugate them in different forms.
2. **Present, Past, and Future Tenses**: Understand how to express actions in different timeframes.
3. **Negative Forms**: Learn to say what you **don't** do.
4. **Polite and Informal Forms**: Understand when to use polite or casual language depending on the situation.

By the end of this chapter, you'll be able to transform basic verb forms into different tenses, make sentences polite or casual, and talk about what you do, did, and will do.

Let's start by laying the foundation with an **Introduction to Verb Conjugation**!

Introduction to Verb Conjugation

In Japanese, verbs are the **heart** of a sentence. Proper conjugation is essential for expressing actions, feelings, and states. Fortunately, Japanese verb conjugation follows a set of consistent patterns that make it easier to master once you learn the basics.

1. Understanding Verb Groups

Japanese verbs are divided into three main groups based on their endings and conjugation patterns:

1. **Group 1 (う-Verbs / Godan Verbs)**
   - These verbs end in a **-u sound** (e.g., う, く, す, つ, ぬ, む, ぶ, る).
   - Examples:
     - かく (*kaku*) – To write

- ■ はなす (*hanasu*) – To speak
- ■ のむ (*nomu*) – To drink

2. **Group 2 (る-Verbs / Ichidan Verbs)**
   - ○ These verbs end in the syllable **-ru**, and the vowel before -ru is **either e or i** (e.g., べる, みる).
   - ○ Examples:
     - ■ たべる (*taberu*) – To eat
     - ■ みる (*miru*) – To see
     - ■ おきる (*okiru*) – To wake up

3. **Group 3 (Irregular Verbs)**
   - ○ There are only two irregular verbs in Japanese:
     - ■ する (*suru*) – To do
     - ■ くる (*kuru*) – To come

Each group follows a different conjugation pattern, but once you learn these patterns, you can conjugate any verb within that group.

2. Basic Conjugation Forms

To start, let's focus on two fundamental conjugations: the **dictionary form** and the **masu-form**.

- **Dictionary Form**: This is the plain, non-polite form used in informal speech and in dictionaries—for example, たべる (*taberu* – to eat) and いく (*iku* – to go).
- **Masu-form**: This is the **polite** form that ends in -ます (*-masu*) and is used in daily conversation. For example:
  - ○ たべます (*tabemasu* – eat)
  - ○ いきます (*ikimasu* – go)

The **dictionary form** is your base form, and all other conjugations (past, negative, etc.) build off of this. Let's see how to create the **-masu form** for each group:

1. **Group 1 (う-Verbs)**
   - ○ Change the **final -u sound** to its corresponding **-i sound** and add **-ます**.
   - ○ Example:
     - ■ のむ (*nomu* – to drink) → のみます (*nomimasu* – drink)
     - ■ かく (*kaku* – to write) → かきます (*kakimasu* – write)

2. **Group 2 (る-Verbs)**
   - ○ Remove the **-ru** ending and add **-ます**.

- Example:
    - たべる (*taberu* – to eat) → **たべます** (*tabemasu* – eat)
    - みる (*miru* – to see) → **みます** (*mimasu* – see)

3. **Group 3 (Irregular Verbs)**
    - These two verbs conjugate differently:
        - する (*suru*) → **します** (*shimasu* – do)
        - くる (*kuru*) → **きます** (*kimasu* – come)

3. Conjugating for Tenses: Present, Past, and Future

In Japanese, the **present tense** and **future tense** share the same conjugation. To express actions that are currently happening or will happen in the future, use the **-masu form**:

- **Present/Future Affirmative**:
    - Group 1: のみます (*nomimasu*) – I drink / I will drink
    - Group 2: みます (*mimasu*) – I see / I will see
    - Group 3: きます (*kimasu*) – I come / I will come

To indicate the **past tense**, change the **-ます** ending to **-ました** (*-mashita*):

- **Past Affirmative**:
    - Group 1: のみました (*nomimashita*) – I drank
    - Group 2: みました (*mimashita*) – I saw
    - Group 3: きました (*kimashita*) – I came

4. Negative Forms

Japanese verbs can also be conjugated to express **negative** actions. To negate the **-masu form**, replace **-ます** with **-ません** (*-masen*). This works for both present and future negative forms:

- **Present/Future Negative**:
    - Group 1: のみません (*nomimasen*) – I don't drink / I won't drink
    - Group 2: みません (*mimasen*) – I don't see / I won't see
    - Group 3: きません (*kimasen*) – I don't come / I won't come

For **past negative** forms, replace **-ました** with **-ませんでした** (*-masen deshita*):

- **Past Negative**:
    - Group 1: のみませんでした (*nomimasen deshita*) – I didn't drink
    - Group 2: みませんでした (*mimasen deshita*) – I didn't see
    - Group 3: きませんでした (*kimasen deshita*) – I didn't come

Tenses: Past, Present, and Future

Understanding how to express actions in different **tenses** is crucial for effective communication in any language. In Japanese, the tense of a verb changes based on the **ending**, and the same basic form can indicate both present and future actions.

In this section, we'll look at how to use verb conjugations to talk about actions that are happening **now**, happened **in the past**, or will happen **in the future**.

Let's explore the core tense patterns in Japanese:

1. Present and Future Tense

In Japanese, the **present** and **future** tenses share the same verb form. This means that the same conjugation can be used to describe both an action that is currently happening and one that will happen in the future.

- **Present/Future Affirmative**: -ます (-*masu*)
  Use this form to express what you do regularly, what is happening now, or what you will do.

Examples:

- 食べます (*tabemasu*) – I eat / I will eat
  - 私はすしを食べます。(*Watashi wa sushi o tabemasu.*)
    Meaning: I eat sushi. (regular action)
  - 明日、私はすしを食べます。(*Ashita, watashi wa sushi o tabemasu.*)
    Meaning: Tomorrow, I will eat sushi. (future action)
- 行きます (*ikimasu*) – I go / I will go
  - 私は学校に行きます。(*Watashi wa gakkou ni ikimasu.*)
    Meaning: I go to school.
  - 週末に図書館に行きます。(*Shuumatsu ni toshokan ni ikimasu.*)
    Meaning: I will go to the library on the weekend.

Tip: If you want to indicate a **future** action clearly, you can add a **time word** such as 明日 (*ashita* – tomorrow) or 来週 (*raishuu* – next week).

2. Past Tense

To express **completed actions**, you need to conjugate the verb into the **past tense**. In the polite form, the -ます (-*masu*) ending changes to -ました (-*mashita*).

- **Past Affirmative**: -ました (-*mashita*)
  Use this form to describe actions that have already happened.

Examples:

- 食べました (*tabemashita*) – I ate
    - 私はすしを食べました。(*Watashi wa sushi o tabemashita.*)
    Meaning: I ate sushi.
- 行きました (*ikimashita*) – I went
    - 私は学校に行きました。(*Watashi wa gakkou ni ikimashita.*)
    Meaning: I went to school.
- 見ました (*mimashita*) – I saw
    - 映画を見ました。(*Eiga o mimashita.*)
    Meaning: I saw a movie.

Tip: The past form always indicates **completed** actions, regardless of when they were done (e.g., yesterday, last week, or a moment ago).

3. Future Intentions

To talk about **intentions** or **plans** for the future, you can use the **present/future tense,** as shown above, but adding context helps. You can include words like:

- つもりです (*tsumori desu*) – I intend to / I plan to
    - 来週、日本に行くつもりです。(*Raishuu, Nihon ni iku tsumori desu.*)
    Meaning: I plan to go to Japan next week.
- 予定です (*yotei desu*) – It is scheduled / I am supposed to
    - 会議は午後2時に始まる予定です。(*Kaigi wa gogo niji ni hajimaru yotei desu.*)
    Meaning: The meeting is scheduled to start at 2 p.m.

4. Negative Forms Across Tenses

To express **negative actions** (things you don't do or didn't do), you need to conjugate the verb accordingly:

- **Present/Future Negative**: -ません (*-masen*)
    - 食べません (*tabemasen*) – I don't eat / I won't eat
    - 私はすしを食べません。(*Watashi wa sushi o tabemasen.*)
    Meaning: I don't eat sushi / I won't eat sushi.
- **Past Negative**: -ませんでした (*-masen deshita*)
    - 食べませんでした (*tabemasen deshita*) – I didn't eat
    - 私はすしを食べませんでした。(*Watashi wa sushi o tabemasen deshita.*)
    Meaning: I didn't eat sushi.

5. Practice Conjugation Chart

Let's review how verbs change across different tenses and forms using the example verbs たべる (*taberu* – to eat) and いく (*iku* – to go):

Verb Form	たべる (taberu)	いく (iku)
Dictionary Form	たべる	いく
Masu Form	たべます	いきます
Present Negative	たべません	いきません
Past Form	たべました	いきました
Past Negative	たべませんでした	いきませんでした

6. Example Sentences for Each Tense

1. **Present Tense**:
   私は毎日水を飲みます。(*Watashi wa mainichi mizu o nomimasu.*)
   Meaning: I drink water every day.

2. **Past Tense**:
   彼は昨日コーヒーを飲みました。(*Kare wa kinou ko-hi- o nomimashita.*)
   Meaning: He drank coffee yesterday.

3. **Future Intention**:
   私は明日図書館に行くつもりです。(*Watashi wa ashita toshokan ni iku tsumori desu.*)
   Meaning: I plan to go to the library tomorrow.

4. **Negative Present Tense**:
   私はお酒を飲みません。(*Watashi wa osake o nomimasen.*)
   Meaning: I don't drink alcohol.

5. **Negative Past Tense**:
   彼女は昼ご飯を食べませんでした。(*Kanojo wa hirugohan o tabemasen deshita.*)
   Meaning: She didn't eat lunch.

Key Takeaways

❖ **Verb conjugation** is essential for expressing actions in Japanese and follows specific patterns based on verb groups (う -Verbs, る -Verbs, and Irregular Verbs).

❖ **Tense** in Japanese is primarily indicated through changes in verb endings:

  ➤ **Present/Future Affirmative**: - ます (*-masu*)

  ➤ **Past Affirmative**: - ました (*-mashita*)

  ➤ **Present/Future Negative**: - ません (*-masen*)

  ➤ **Past Negative**: - ませんでした (*-masen deshita*)

❖ The same form is used for both **present** and **future tense**; context and time expressions (e.g., 明日 - *ashita* - tomorrow) help clarify the meaning.

❖ **Negative forms** are created by replacing the affirmative ending with - ません for present/future or - ませんでした for the past.

❖ Understanding verb groups is key to correctly applying conjugation patterns:

  ➤ **Group 1 (う -Verbs)**: Change the final -u sound to the corresponding -i sound.

  ➤ **Group 2 (る -Verbs)**: Simply drop the - る and add the new ending.

  ➤ **Irregular Verbs**: Memorize their unique patterns (する becomes します; くる becomes きます).

Exercises

Exercise 1: Conjugation Practice

Convert the following verbs into their **-ます** form, **past** form, **negative** form, and **past negative** form:

Dictionary Form	Masu Form	Past Form	Negative Form	Past Negative Form
読む (*yomu*) – to read				
食べる (*taberu*) – to eat				
話す (*hanasu*) – to speak				
行く (*iku*) – to go				
する (*suru*) – to do				

Exercise 2: Translate the Sentences

Translate the following sentences into Japanese using the correct verb conjugation:

1. I eat breakfast every day.
2. She didn't go to the supermarket yesterday.
3. He drinks coffee in the morning.
4. We will study Japanese tomorrow.
5. They didn't watch the movie last week.

Exercise 3: Sentence Expansion Practice

Expand the following sentences by adding **time expressions** and **negating** the actions:

1. 彼はりんごを食べます。

   Kare wa ringo o tabemasu.
    - Meaning: He eats an apple.
    - Expanded: He doesn't eat an apple **in the morning**.

2. 私は図書館に行きます。

   Watashi wa toshokan ni ikimasu.

- o Meaning: I go to the library.
    - o Expanded: I will go to the library **tomorrow afternoon**.

3. 彼女は本を読みました。
   Kanojo wa hon o yomimashita.
    - o Meaning: She read a book.
    - o Expanded: She didn't read a book **last night**.

4. 私たちはコーヒーを飲みます。
   Watashitachi wa ko-hi- o nomimasu.
    - o Meaning: We drink coffee.
    - o Expanded: We won't drink coffee **next week**.

5. 彼らは日本に行きました。
   Karera wa Nihon ni ikimashita.
    - o Meaning: They went to Japan.
    - o Expanded: They didn't go to Japan **last summer**.

Exercise 4: Fill in the Blanks
Choose the correct conjugation to complete the sentences:

1. 彼は昨日映画を＿＿＿＿＿。 (*Kare wa kinou eiga o ＿＿＿＿＿.*) – He watched a movie yesterday.
    - o Options: 見ます (*mimasu*), 見ました (*mimashita*), 見ませんでした (*mimasen deshita*)

2. 私は毎日お茶を＿＿＿＿＿。 (*Watashi wa mainichi ocha o ＿＿＿＿＿.*) – I drink tea every day.
    - o Options: 飲みました (*nomimashita*), 飲みません (*nomimasen*), 飲みます (*nomimasu*)

3. 彼女は昨日学校に＿＿＿＿＿。 (*Kanojo wa kinou gakkou ni ＿＿＿＿＿.*) – She didn't go to school yesterday.
    - o Options: 行きます (*ikimasu*), 行きません (*ikimasen*), 行きませんでした (*ikimasen deshita*)

4. 私たちは図書館で勉強を＿＿＿＿＿。 (*Watashitachi wa toshokan de benkyou o ＿＿＿＿＿.*) – We will study at the library.
    - o Options: します (*shimasu*), しませんでした (*shimasen deshita*), しました (*shimashita*)

5. 彼は来週日本に＿＿＿＿＿。 (*Kare wa raishuu Nihon ni ＿＿＿＿＿.*) – He will go to Japan next week.
    - o Options: 行きません (*ikimasen*), 行きます (*ikimasu*), 行きました (*ikimashita*).

Answer Key

Exercise 1: Conjugation Practice

Dictionary Form	Masu Form	Past Form	Negative Form	Past Negative Form
読む (*yomu*)	よみます (*yomimasu*)	よみました (*yomimashita*)	よみません (*yomimasen*)	よみませんでした (*yomimasen deshita*)
食べる (*taberu*)	たべます (*tabemasu*)	たべました (*tabemashita*)	たべません (*tabemasen*)	たべませんでした (*tabemasen deshita*)
話す (*hanasu*)	はなします (*hanashimasu*)	はなしました (*hanashimashita*)	はなしません (*hanashimasen*)	はなしませんでした (*hanashimasen deshita*)
行く (*iku*)	いきます (*ikimasu*)	いきました (*ikimashita*)	いきません (*ikimasen*)	いきませんでした (*ikimasen deshita*)
する (*suru*)	します (*shimasu*)	しました (*shimashita*)	しません (*shimasen*)	しませんでした (*shimasen deshita*)

Exercise 2: Translate the Sentences

1. **I eat breakfast every day.**
   毎日朝ごはんを食べます。(Mainichi asagohan o tabemasu.)

2. **She didn't go to the supermarket yesterday.**
   彼女は昨日スーパーに行きませんでした。(Kanojo wa kinou su-pa- ni ikimasen deshita.)

3. **He drinks coffee in the morning.**
   彼は朝にコーヒーを飲みます。(Kare wa asa ni ko-hi- o nomimasu.)

4. **We will study Japanese tomorrow.**
   私たちは明日日本語を勉強します。(Watashitachi wa ashita nihongo o benkyou shimasu.)

5. **They didn't watch the movie last week.**
彼らは先週映画を見ませんでした。(Karera wa senshuu eiga o mimasen deshita.)

Exercise 3: Sentence Expansion Practice

1. 彼はりんごを食べます。
   Expanded: 彼は朝にりんごを食べません。
   (Kare wa asa ni ringo o tabemasen.) – He doesn't eat an apple in the morning.

2. 私は図書館に行きます。
   Expanded: 私は明日の午後図書館に行きます。
   (Watashi wa ashita no gogo toshokan ni ikimasu.) – I will go to the library tomorrow afternoon.

3. 彼女は本を読みました。
   Expanded: 彼女は昨晩本を読みませんでした。
   (Kanojo wa sakuban hon o yomimasen deshita.) – She didn't read a book last night.

4. 私たちはコーヒーを飲みます。
   Expanded: 私たちは来週コーヒーを飲みません。
   (Watashitachi wa raishuu ko-hi- o nomimasen.) – We won't drink coffee next week.

5. 彼らは日本に行きました。
   Expanded: 彼らは去年の夏に日本に行きませんでした。
   (Karera wa kyonen no natsu ni Nihon ni ikimasen deshita.) – They didn't go to Japan last summer.

Exercise 4: Fill in the Blanks

1. Correct Answer: 見ました

2. Correct Answer: 飲みます

3. Correct Answer: 行きませんでした

4. Correct Answer: します

5. Correct Answer: 行きます

Chapter 4: Expanding Vocabulary Through Themes

"To have another language is to possess a second soul."
– Charlemagne

Vocabulary is more than just a collection of words—it's a key to understanding a language's culture and context. In this chapter, we'll explore how to build your vocabulary using **thematic groups** that reflect everyday scenarios. By focusing on words and phrases for specific themes, you'll be able to navigate common situations like **shopping**, **dining out**, and **getting around** in Japanese-speaking environments.

We'll break down this chapter into two primary sections:

1. **Shopping, Food, and Dining Vocabulary**
   You'll learn essential words and expressions to **shop for goods**, **order food**, and **dine out**. This includes everything from asking for prices to describing food preferences. By mastering these terms, you'll be able to shop confidently and enjoy dining experiences without language barriers.

2. **Asking for Directions and Getting Around**
   Traveling and exploring a new place can be both exciting and challenging. This section will equip you with the vocabulary needed to **ask for directions**, **navigate public transportation**, and **describe locations**. You'll practice phrases for asking where something is, giving directions, and using key location-based words.

Each section will provide **targeted vocabulary**, example phrases, and simple dialogue practice. This approach will help you learn how to use these words in real-world settings, making your communication more practical and effective.

By the end of this chapter, you'll have a versatile vocabulary set for shopping, dining, and navigating your surroundings, which will empower you to interact more confidently in various everyday situations.

Let's get started!

Shopping, Food, and Dining Vocabulary

Shopping and dining are some of the most common activities you'll encounter when traveling or living in Japan. Knowing the right words and expressions will make these experiences much more enjoyable and less stressful.

Let's begin by building a strong set of words and expressions for **shopping**, followed by **food-related vocabulary**, and finally, key phrases for **ordering and dining**.

1. Vocabulary for Shopping

Whether you're browsing through a department store or picking up groceries, having a grasp of basic shopping terms is essential. Here are some key words and phrases to help you get started:

Japanese	Romaji	Meaning
店	*mise*	Store / Shop
スーパー	*su-pa-*	Supermarket
デパート	*depa-to*	Department store
市場	*ichiba*	Market
服	*fuku*	Clothes
値段	*nedan*	Price
安い	*yasui*	Cheap
高い	*takai*	Expensive
セール	*se-ru*	Sale
サイズ	*saizu*	Size
試着する	*shichaku suru*	To try on (clothes)
現金	*genkin*	Cash
クレジットカード	*kurejitto ka-do*	Credit card
領収書	*ryoushuusho*	Receipt
店員	*tenin*	Shop clerk / Employee

Example Phrases:

- これはいくらですか？ (*Kore wa ikura desu ka?*)
  Meaning: How much is this?

- サイズがありますか？ (*Saizu ga arimasu ka?*)
  Meaning: Do you have this in another size?

- 試着してもいいですか？ (*Shichaku shitemo ii desu ka?*)
  Meaning: May I try this on?

- クレジットカードは使えますか？ (*Kurejitto ka-do wa tsukaemasu ka?*)
  Meaning: Can I use a credit card?

2. Food and Ingredients Vocabulary

Understanding food-related vocabulary will help you read menus, buy ingredients, and talk about your favorite dishes. Here are some everyday food items and phrases you'll likely encounter:

Category	Japanese	Romaji	Meaning
Vegetables	野菜	*yasai*	Vegetables
Fruits	果物	*kudamono*	Fruits
Meat	肉	*niku*	Meat
Fish	魚	*sakana*	Fish
Rice	ご飯	*gohan*	Rice
Bread	パン	*pan*	Bread
Noodles	麺	*men*	Noodles
Egg	卵	*tamago*	Egg
Water	水	*mizu*	Water
Tea	お茶	*ocha*	Tea

Coffee	コーヒー	*ko-hi-*	Coffee
Juice	ジュース	*ju-su*	Juice
Sweets	お菓子	*okashi*	Sweets / Snacks

Example Phrases:

- 野菜をください。(*Yasai o kudasai.*)
  Meaning: Please give me some vegetables.
- 肉と魚はありますか？(*Niku to sakana wa arimasu ka?*)
  Meaning: Do you have meat and fish?
- パンを二つください。(*Pan o futatsu kudasai.*)
  Meaning: Please give me two pieces of bread.

3. Dining Out: Ordering and Common Phrases

When dining out, understanding menu items and placing an order can be challenging without the right vocabulary. Let's look at some key phrases to help you order food and interact with restaurant staff.

Common Restaurant Vocabulary:

Japanese	Romaji	Meaning
メニュー	*menyuu*	Menu
注文	*chuumon*	Order
ウェイター / ウェイトレス	*ueitaa / ueitoresu*	Waiter / Waitress
飲み物	*nomimono*	Drink
おすすめ	*osusume*	Recommendation
前菜	*zensai*	Appetizer
主菜	*shusai*	Main dish

| デザート | *deza-to* | Dessert |
| ごちそうさまでした | *gochisousama deshita* | Thank you for the meal |

Example Phrases for Ordering:

- 注文をお願いします。 (*Chuumon o onegaishimasu.*)
  Meaning: I would like to order, please.

- おすすめは何ですか？ (*Osusume wa nan desu ka?*)
  Meaning: What do you recommend?

- ビールを一つください。 (*Bi-ru o hitotsu kudasai.*)
  Meaning: Please give me one beer.

- 水をください。 (*Mizu o kudasai.*)
  Meaning: Please give me some water.

Polite Expressions for Dining:

- いただきます (*Itadakimasu*)
  Meaning: Used before eating to express gratitude and respect for the food and those who prepared it. ごちそうさまでした (*Gochisousama deshita*)
  Meaning: Used after finishing a meal to express appreciation

Example Dialogue: At a Restaurant

Here's a sample dialogue to illustrate how these words and phrases come together in a real dining scenario:

– **Customer**: おすすめは何ですか？ (*Osusume wa nan desu ka?*)
Meaning: What do you recommend?

– **Waiter**: おすすめはカツ丼です。 (*Osusume wa katsudon desu.*)
Meaning: I recommend the pork cutlet rice bowl.

– **Customer**: じゃあ、カツ丼をください。 (*Jaa, katsudon o kudasai.*)
Meaning: Then, I'll have the pork cutlet rice bowl, please.

– **Waiter**: 飲み物はどうしますか？ (*Nomimono wa dou shimasu ka?*)
Meaning: What would you like to drink?

– **Customer**: 水をお願いします。 (*Mizu o onegaishimasu.*)
Meaning: Water, please.

Asking for Directions and Getting Around

When you're in an unfamiliar place, the ability to ask for directions and understand responses is invaluable.

Let's get started by building your vocabulary for **locations** and **directions**!

1. Essential Vocabulary for Directions and Locations

Here's a list of words and phrases you'll need to describe locations, directions, and common places:

Location Words:

Japanese	Romaji	Meaning
ここ	*koko*	Here
そこ	*soko*	There
あそこ	*asoko*	Over there
どこ	*doko*	Where?
右	*migi*	Right
左	*hidari*	Left
前	*mae*	Front / Before
後ろ	*ushiro*	Behind
中	*naka*	Inside
外	*soto*	Outside
上	*ue*	Above / Up
下	*shita*	Below / Down

隣	*tonari*	Next to
向かい	*mukai*	Opposite / Across
近い	*chikai*	Near / Close
遠い	*tooi*	Far

Example Sentences:

- 駅はどこですか？ (*Eki wa doko desu ka?*)
  Meaning: Where is the train station?
- あなたの右にあります。 (*Anata no migi ni arimasu.*)
  Meaning: It's on your right.
- コンビニは銀行の隣です。 (*Konbini wa ginkou no tonari desu.*)
  Meaning: The convenience store is next to the bank.

2. Asking for Directions Politely

When asking for directions, it's important to use polite language. Let's look at some common phrases to help you ask and understand directions effectively.

Basic Phrases for Asking Directions:

Japanese	Romaji	Meaning
〜はどこですか？	*〜 wa doko desu ka?*	Where is 〜?
〜に行きたいです。	*〜 ni ikitai desu.*	I want to go to 〜.
〜へ行くにはどうすればいいですか？	*〜 e iku ni wa dou sureba ii desu ka?*	How do I get to 〜?
この辺に〜はありますか？	*Kono hen ni 〜 wa arimasu ka?*	Is there a 〜 around here?
すみません、〜までの行き方を教えてください。	*Sumimasen, 〜 made no ikikata o oshiete kudasai.*	Excuse me, can you tell me how to get to 〜?

Example Dialogues:

- **Person A**: すみません、駅はどこですか？ (*Sumimasen, eki wa doko desu ka?*)
  Meaning: Excuse me, where is the train station?
- **Person B**: 駅はあそこです。 (*Eki wa asoko desu.*)
  Meaning: The station is over there.
- **Person A**: この道をまっすぐ行ってください。 (*Kono michi o massugu itte kudasai.*)
  Meaning: Please go straight down this road.

Other Helpful Phrases:

- 右に曲がってください。 (*Migi ni magatte kudasai.*)
  Meaning: Please turn right.
- 左に曲がります。 (*Hidari ni magarimasu.*)
  Meaning: I'll turn left.
- この道をまっすぐ行ってください。 (*Kono michi o massugu itte kudasai.*)
  Meaning: Please go straight down this road.

3. Navigating Public Transportation

Japan is known for its efficient public transportation system, including **trains**, **buses**, and **taxis**. Understanding key terms and phrases will help you get around more easily. Let's look at some common terms you'll need to navigate the transportation system:

Train and Bus Vocabulary:

Japanese	Romaji	Meaning
駅	*eki*	Station
電車	*densha*	Train
地下鉄	*chikatetsu*	Subway
バス	*basu*	Bus
バス停	*basutei*	Bus stop
改札	*kaisatsu*	Ticket gate

乗り換え	*norikae*	Transfer
終点	*shuuten*	Last stop
行き	*yuki*	Bound for
乗車券	*joushaken*	Passenger ticket
定期券	*teikiken*	Commuter pass
運賃	*unchin*	Fare
どの電車	*dono densha*	Which train?
～行き	*~ yuki*	Bound for ~

Example Phrases for Train and Bus Travel:

- これは東京行きですか？ (*Kore wa Tokyo yuki desu ka?*)
  Meaning: Is this train bound for Tokyo?

- どの電車に乗りますか？ (*Dono densha ni norimasu ka?*)
  Meaning: Which train should I take?

- 乗り換えはどこですか？ (*Norikae wa doko desu ka?*)
  Meaning: Where is the transfer station?

- 次の駅は何ですか？ (*Tsugi no eki wa nan desu ka?*)
  Meaning: What is the next station?

4. Using Taxis

If you're taking a taxi, knowing some key phrases will help you communicate with the driver. Here are some basic terms and expressions for using taxis:

Taxi Vocabulary and Phrases:

Japanese	Romaji	Meaning
タクシー	*takushii*	Taxi
運転手	*untenshu*	Driver
～までお願いします。	*~ made onegaishimasu.*	To ~, please.
ここで止めてください。	*Koko de tomete kudasai.*	Please stop here.
いくらですか？	*Ikura desu ka?*	How much is it?
領収書をください。	*Ryoushuusho o kudasai.*	Please give me a receipt.

Example Dialogue:

- **Customer**: 渋谷までお願いします。 (*Shibuya made onegaishimasu.*)
  Meaning: To Shibuya, please.
- **Driver**: はい、渋谷までですね。 (*Hai, Shibuya made desu ne.*)
  Meaning: Okay, to Shibuya.
- **Customer**: ここで止めてください。 (*Koko de tomete kudasai.*)
  Meaning: Please stop here.

Key Takeaways

❖ Learn key phrases like "How much is this?" (これはいくらですか？) and "I would like to order" (注文をお願いします).

❖ Use directional words like 右 (*migi* - right), 左 (*hidari* - left), and どこ (*doko* - where) to navigate unfamiliar places.

❖ Understand terms like 駅 (*eki* - station), 電車 (*densha* - train), and 乗り換え (*norikae* - transfer) to get around easily.

❖ Simple expressions like 渋谷までお願いします (*Shibuya made onegaishimasu* - To Shibuya, please) can help you communicate with drivers.

Exercises

Exercise 1: Vocabulary Matching

Match the Japanese words to their English meanings:

1. 駅 → ___
2. 近い → ___
3. 服 → ___
4. 左 → ___
5. 市場 → ___
6. 魚 → ___
7. デパート → ___
8. 遠い → ___
9. ここ → ___
10. 隣 → ___

Options:

A. Market
B. Train Station
C. Near
D. There
E. Far
F. Clothes
G. Fish
H. Department Store
I. Here
J. Next to

Exercise 2: Fill in the Blanks

Complete the following sentences with the correct location or direction word:

1. スーパーは______にあります。 (*The supermarket is on the left.*)

   ○ Options: 左, 右

2. 銀行は本屋の______です。 (*The bank is next to the bookstore.*)

   ○ Options: 向かい, 隣

3. レストランはあのビルの______です。 (*The restaurant is inside that building.*)

○ Options: 外, 中

4. バス停はどこですか？ ＿＿＿＿＿ですか？ (*Where is the bus stop? Is it near?*)

   ○ Options: 近い, 遠い

5. 駅は＿＿＿＿＿の向かいです。 (*The station is across from the park.*)

   ○ Options: 公園, 銀行

Exercise 3: Translate the Sentences

Translate the following sentences into Japanese:

1. Where is the convenience store?
2. Please go straight and turn right.
3. I want to go to the train station.
4. How much is this book?
5. The restaurant is on the left.

Exercise 4: Role Play Practice

Imagine you're at a restaurant and want to order food. Using what you've learned, create a short dialogue where you ask for a recommendation, place an order, and request a drink. Use at least 3 of the phrases from the chapter.

Answer Key

Exercise 1: Vocabulary Matching

1. 駅 → B. Train Station
2. 近い → C. Near
3. 服 → F. Clothes
4. 左 → D. Left
5. 市場 → A. Market
6. 魚 → G. Fish
7. デパート → H. Department Store
8. 遠い → E. Far
9. ここ → I. Here
10. 隣 → J. Next to

Exercise 2: Fill in the Blanks

1. スーパーは左にあります。 (*Supermarket is on the left.*)
2. 銀行は本屋の隣です。 (*The bank is next to the bookstore.*)
3. レストランはあのビルの中です。 (*The restaurant is inside that building.*)
4. バス停はどこですか？近いですか？ (*Is it near?*)
5. 駅は公園の向かいです。 (*The station is across from the park.*)

Exercise 3: Translate the Sentences

1. コンビニはどこですか？ (*Konbini wa doko desu ka?*)
2. まっすぐ行って、右に曲がってください。 (*Massugu itte, migi ni magatte kudasai.*)
3. 駅に行きたいです。 (*Eki ni ikitai desu.*)
4. この本はいくらですか？ (*Kono hon wa ikura desu ka?*)
5. レストランは左にあります。 (*Resutoran wa hidari ni arimasu.*)

Exercise 4: Role Play Practice

- **Customer**: おすすめは何ですか？ (*Osusume wa nan desu ka?*)
  Meaning: What do you recommend?
- **Waiter**: おすすめはカレーです。 (*Osusume wa kare- desu.*)
  Meaning: I recommend curry.

- **Customer**: じゃあ、カレーをください。(*Jaa, kare- o kudasai.*)
  Meaning: Then, I'll have the curry, please.

- **Waiter**: 飲み物はどうしますか？ (*Nomimono wa dou shimasu ka?*)
  Meaning: What would you like to drink?

- **Customer**: お水をください。 (*Omizu o kudasai.*)
  Meaning: Water, please.

Chapter 5: Practical Conversations for Beginners

"Communication works for those who work at it."
— John Powell

Knowing words and phrases is the foundation of language learning, but using them effectively in conversations is where real progress happens. In this chapter, we'll focus on **practical conversation skills** to help you feel more comfortable engaging in basic interactions in Japanese. From **introducing yourself** and **asking questions** to **making small talk**, you'll learn how to express yourself and build connections with others.

We'll begin by covering simple greetings and self-introductions, move on to common phrases used in everyday interactions, and then dive into basic **question patterns** that will enable you to ask for information and keep a conversation flowing.

This chapter will focus on:

1. **Introducing Yourself and Asking Questions**: Learn the essentials for talking about who you are, where you're from, and what you do. You'll also practice asking common questions such as "What's your name?" and "Where are you from?"

2. **Small Talk and Simple Dialogue Practice**: Master brief conversations that will help you handle everyday situations, like discussing the weather, talking about hobbies, or making polite requests.

By the end of this chapter, you'll have the confidence to start basic conversations, respond to common questions, and interact politely in various settings. Let's start by learning how to **introduce yourself and ask basic questions**!

Introducing Yourself and Asking Questions

Introducing yourself is one of the first and most important skills when learning a new language. In Japanese, self-introductions are generally polite and follow a specific format.

1. Self-Introduction Vocabulary and Phrases

A typical self-introduction in Japanese usually follows a set sequence of information: **name**, **origin**, **occupation**, and a **polite closing**. Here's a step-by-step guide with phrases and expressions:

Japanese	Romaji	Meaning
はじめまして	*Hajimemashite*	Nice to meet you (first time only).

私は〜です。	*Watashi wa ~ desu.*	I am ~.
〜と申します。	*~ to moushimasu.*	My name is ~ (more polite)
アメリカ出身です。	*Amerika shusshin desu.*	I'm from the USA.
日本人です。	*Nihonjin desu.*	I'm Japanese.
学生です。	*Gakusei desu.*	I'm a student.
会社員です。	*Kaishain desu.*	I'm a company employee.
よろしくお願いします。	*Yoroshiku onegaishimasu*	Please treat me well / Pleased to meet you.

2. Building a Self-Introduction

Let's put these elements together to create a full self-introduction. Here's a basic example:

Example 1: Basic Introduction

はじめまして。
私の名前はジョンです。
アメリカ出身です。
学生です。
よろしくお願いします。

Romaji:
Hajimemashite.
Watashi no namae wa Jon desu.
Amerika shusshin desu.
Gakusei desu.
Yoroshiku onegaishimasu.

Meaning:
Hello, nice to meet you.
My name is John.
I'm from the United States.
I'm a student.
Pleased to meet you.

Let's break it down:

- はじめまして (*hajimemashite*) is a greeting used when meeting someone for the first time.
- 私の名前は ～ です (*watashi no namae wa ~ desu*) means "My name is ~." Replace "ジョン" (*Jon*) with your own name.
- ～出身です (*~ shusshin desu*) tells the listener where you're from. Replace "アメリカ" (*Amerika*) with your country of origin.
- よろしくお願いします (*yoroshiku onegaishimasu*) is a polite closing phrase that doesn't translate directly but means something like "Please treat me favorably."

Note: In casual settings, you can simplify your self-introduction by omitting formal expressions like *yoroshiku onegaishimasu*.

3. Asking Basic Questions

After introducing yourself, asking the other person about themselves is polite. Here are some key questions you can use to continue the conversation:

Japanese	Romaji	Meaning
お名前は何ですか？	*Onamae wa nan desu ka?*	What's your name?
どこ出身ですか？	*Doko shusshin desu ka?*	Where are you from?
何をしていますか？	*Nani o shiteimasu ka?*	What do you do? / What are you doing?
何歳ですか？	*Nansai desu ka?*	How old are you?
お仕事は何ですか？	*Oshigoto wa nan desu ka?*	What is your job?
趣味は何ですか？	*Shumi wa nan desu ka?*	What are your hobbies?

Example Questions in Conversation:

- **Person A**: お名前は何ですか？ (*Onamae wa nan desu ka?*)
  Meaning: What's your name?
- **Person B**: 私の名前はサラです。 (*Watashi no namae wa Sara desu.*)
  Meaning: My name is Sara.

- **Person A**: どこ出身ですか？ (*Doko shusshin desu ka?*)
  Meaning: Where are you from?
- **Person B**: イギリス出身です。 (*Igirisu shusshin desu.*)
  Meaning: I'm from the UK.

4. Using Polite Question Structures

In Japanese, the particle **か (ka)** is added to the end of a statement to turn it into a question:

- **Statement**: あなたは学生です。 (*Anata wa gakusei desu.*)
  Meaning: You are a student.
- **Question**: あなたは学生ですか？ (*Anata wa gakusei desu ka?*)
  Meaning: Are you a student?

You can use this pattern to create questions from almost any statement.

Example:

- あなたは日本人です。 (*Anata wa Nihonjin desu.*)
  - You are Japanese.
- あなたは日本人ですか？ (*Anata wa Nihonjin desu ka?*)
  - Are you Japanese?

5. Sharing Personal Information

To share more about yourself, use the following patterns:

1. **Talking About Age**
   - 私は２５歳です。 (*Watashi wa nijuugo sai desu.*)
     Meaning: I am 25 years old.
2. **Talking About Occupation**
   - 会社員です。 (*Kaishain desu.*)
     Meaning: I am a company employee.
3. **Talking About Hobbies**
   - 私の趣味は読書です。 (*Watashi no shumi wa dokusho desu.*)
     Meaning: My hobby is reading.

Small Talk and Simple Dialogue Practice

Once you've introduced yourself, it's natural to move on to **small talk**—those simple, everyday conversations that help build rapport and maintain friendly interaction.

Let's look at some common topics and example dialogues.

1. Talking About the Weather

Discussing the weather is a universal way to start a conversation. Here are some basic phrases to talk about the weather in Japanese:

Japanese	Romaji	Meaning
今日はいい天気ですね。	*Kyou wa ii tenki desu ne.*	The weather is nice today, isn't it?
暑いですね。	*Atsui desu ne.*	It's hot, isn't it?
寒いですね。	*Samui desu ne.*	It's cold, isn't it?
雨が降っていますね。	*Ame ga futteimasu ne.*	It's raining, isn't it?

Example Dialogue:

- **Person A**: 今日はいい天気ですね。 (*Kyou wa ii tenki desu ne.*)
  Meaning: The weather is nice today, isn't it?
- **Person B**: はい、気持ちがいいですね。 (*Hai, kimochi ga ii desu ne.*)
  Meaning: Yes, it feels great, doesn't it?

2. Asking About Hobbies

Talking about **hobbies** is a great way to learn more about someone and share your interests. Here's how to ask and answer about hobbies:

Japanese	Romaji	Meaning
趣味は何ですか？	*Shumi wa nan desu ka?*	What are your hobbies?
私の趣味は～です。	*Watashi no shumi wa ~ desu.*	My hobby is ~.
スポーツが好きですか？	*Supo-tsu ga suki desu ka?*	Do you like sports?
音楽が好きです。	*Ongaku ga suki desu.*	I like music.

Example Dialogue:

- **Person A**: 趣味は何ですか？ (*Shumi wa nan desu ka?*)
  Meaning: What are your hobbies?
- **Person B**: 私の趣味は読書です。 (*Watashi no shumi wa dokusho desu.*)
  Meaning: My hobby is reading.
- **Person A**: いいですね。 (*Ii desu ne.*)
  Meaning: That's nice.

3. Asking Simple Questions

Knowing how to ask simple questions is vital to keeping the conversation going. Here are some common questions and ways to respond:

Japanese	Romaji	Meaning
今日はどうですか？	*Kyou wa dou desu ka?*	How is your day?
元気ですか？	*Genki desu ka?*	How are you?
何をしていますか？	*Nani o shiteimasu ka?*	What are you doing?
どこに住んでいますか？	*Doko ni sundeimasu ka?*	Where do you live?

Example Dialogue:

- **Person A**: 元気ですか？ (*Genki desu ka?*)
  Meaning: How are you?
- **Person B**: はい、元気です。あなたは？ (*Hai, genki desu. Anata wa?*)
  Meaning: Yes, I'm fine. And you?
- **Person A**: 私も元気です。 (*Watashi mo genki desu.*)
  Meaning: I'm fine too.

4. Giving and Responding to Compliments

In Japanese, it's common to use compliments to show appreciation or break the ice. Here are some useful phrases and polite responses:

Japanese	Romaji	Meaning
上手ですね。	*Jouzu desu ne.*	You're good at it, aren't you?
きれいですね。	*Kirei desu ne.*	It's beautiful, isn't it?
かわいいですね。	*Kawaii desu ne.*	It's cute, isn't it?
ありがとうございます。	*Arigatou gozaimasu.*	Thank you.

Example Dialogue:

- **Person A**: 日本語が上手ですね。 (*Nihongo ga jouzu desu ne.*)
  Meaning: Your Japanese is good, isn't it?
- **Person B**: ありがとうございます。 (*Arigatou gozaimasu.*)
  Meaning: Thank you.
- **Person A**: どれくらい勉強しましたか？ (*Dore kurai benkyou shimashita ka?*)
  Meaning: How long have you been studying?
- **Person B**: 3年くらいです。 (*San-nen kurai desu.*)
  Meaning: About three years.

5. *Simple Dialogue Practice: Ordering at a Café*

Here's a short dialogue for ordering at a café. Practice using polite expressions and vocabulary:

– **Customer**: コーヒーをお願いします。(*Ko-hi- o onegaishimasu.*)
Meaning: Coffee, please.

– **Waiter**: 砂糖とミルクはどうしますか？(*Satou to miruku wa dou shimasu ka?*)
Meaning: How about sugar and milk?

– **Customer**: 砂糖を少しください。ミルクはいりません。(*Satou o sukoshi kudasai. Miruku wa irimasen.*)
Meaning: A little sugar, please. I don't need milk.

– **Waiter**: かしこまりました。(*Kashikomarimashita.*)
Meaning: Certainly.

– **Customer**: いくらですか？(*Ikura desu ka?*)
Meaning: How much is it?

– **Waiter**: ３００円です。(*Sanbyaku en desu.*)
Meaning: It's 300 yen.

Key Takeaways

❖ Learn essential phrases such as "What's your name?" (お名前は何ですか？) and "I'm from..." (私は...出身です).

❖ Use phrases like "Nice to meet you" (はじめまして) and "Please treat me well" (よろしくお願いします) for polite introductions.

❖ Familiarize yourself with questions like "What do you do?" (何をしていますか？) and "What are your hobbies?" (趣味は何ですか？) to engage others in conversation.

❖ Discuss everyday topics such as the weather (今日はいい天気ですね - The weather is nice today, isn't it?) and hobbies to maintain friendly interactions.

Exercises

Exercise 1: Vocabulary Matching

Match the Japanese phrases to their English meanings:

1. はじめまして → ＿＿
2. 趣味は何ですか？ → ＿＿
3. どこ出身ですか？ → ＿＿
4. よろしくお願いします → ＿＿
5. 今日はいい天気ですね → ＿＿

Options:

A. What are your hobbies??
B. Please treat me well.
C. Nice to meet you.
D. Where are you from?
E. The weather is nice today, isn't it?

Exercise 2: Fill in the Blanks

Complete the sentences with the correct phrases from the chapter:

1. 私の名前は＿＿です。(My name is ＿＿.) Options: ジョン, アンナ
2. あなたは＿＿ですか？(Are you ＿＿?)
   Options: 学生, 会社員
3. 趣味は＿＿です。(My hobby is ＿＿.) Options: 音楽, 映画鑑賞
4. お名前は＿＿ですか？(What's your name?) Options: 何, どちら
5. よろしく＿＿。(Please treat me well.) Options: お願いします, ありがとう

Exercise 3: Translate the Sentences

Translate the following sentences into Japanese:

1. What is your name?
2. Where are you from?
3. What do you do?
4. How are you?
5. My hobby is reading.

Answer Key

Answer to Exercise 1: Vocabulary Matching

1. はじめまして → C. Nice to meet you.

2. 趣味は何ですか？ → A. What are your hobbies??

3. どこ出身ですか？ → D. Where are you from?

4. よろしくお願いします → B. Please treat me well.

5. 今日はいい天気ですね → E. The weather is nice today, isn't it?

Answer to Exercise 2: Fill in the Blanks

1. 私の名前は**ジョン**です。(My name is John.)

2. あなたは**学生**ですか？(Are you a student?)

3. 趣味は**音楽**です。(My hobby is music.)

4. お名前は何ですか？(What's your name?)

5. よろしく**お願いします**。(Please treat me well.)

Answer to Exercise 3: Translate the Sentences

1. お名前は何ですか？ (Onamae wa nan desu ka?)

2. どこ出身ですか？ (Doko shusshin desu ka?)

3. 何をしていますか？ (Nani o shiteimasu ka?)

4. 元気ですか？ (Genki desu ka?)

5. 私の趣味は読書です。 (Watashi no shumi wa dokusho desu.)

Chapter 6: Describing Objects and Situations

> *"A word after a word after a word is power."*
> – Margaret Atwood

Being able to **describe** the world around you is a critical language skill. In Japanese, adjectives and adverbs are the tools you'll use to add color and detail to your conversations. With these words, you can talk about **people, objects, places**, and **situations** more vividly, helping you express your thoughts and emotions accurately.

This chapter will focus on using **adjectives** and **adverbs** to describe size, shape, color, and other characteristics, as well as making **comparisons** between people or things. Understanding how to use descriptive language correctly will make your speech more engaging and dynamic.

We'll start by covering the basic **types of adjectives** in Japanese, learn how to modify sentences with **adverbs**, and finally, we'll look at **comparison structures** to help you express similarities and differences.

Let's get started by learning how to use **adjectives and adverbs** to bring your sentences to life!

Using Adjectives and Adverbs

Adjectives and adverbs add essential details to your sentences, allowing you to express not just what something is but *how* it is. In Japanese, adjectives describe **nouns** (e.g., "a beautiful flower"), while adverbs modify **verbs, adjectives, and other adverbs** (e.g., "quickly run" or "very beautiful").

1. Types of Adjectives in Japanese

Japanese adjectives are divided into **two main categories**: い-adjectives and な-adjectives. Knowing how to differentiate and conjugate these will allow you to describe a variety of things accurately.

い-Adjectives

- **い-adjectives** end in い (e.g., あたらしい - new). They can be directly attached to nouns and conjugated to show different tenses and negations.

Examples:

- 大きい (*ookii*) – Big
- 小さい (*chiisai*) – Small
- 高い (*takai*) – Tall / Expensive
- 面白い (*omoshiroi*) – Interesting

Example Sentences:

- 大きい家です。 (*Ookii ie desu.*)
  Meaning: It's a big house.
- この本は面白いです。 (*Kono hon wa omoshiroi desu.*)
  Meaning: This book is interesting.

Key Conjugation Patterns for い-Adjectives:

Form	Japanese	Romaji	Meaning
Present Positive	大きいです	*ookii desu*	It is big.
Present Negative	大きくないです	*ookiku nai desu*	It is not big.
Past Positive	大きかったです	*ookikatta desu*	It was big.
Past Negative	大きくなかったです	*ookiku nakatta desu*	It was not big.

な-Adjectives

- **な-adjectives** end in a variety of sounds, but they always require the particle **な** when directly modifying a noun (e.g., *きれいな* - beautiful).

Examples:

- 静かな (*shizukana*) – Quiet
- 有名な (*yuumeina*) – Famous
- 便利な (*benrina*) – Convenient
- 元気な (*genkina*) – Energetic

Example Sentences:

- きれいな花です。 (*Kireina hana desu.*)
  Meaning: It's a beautiful flower.
- 便利な場所です。 (*Benrina basho desu.*)
  Meaning: It's a convenient place.

Key Conjugation Patterns for な-Adjectives:

Form	Japanese	Romaji	Meaning
Present Positive	静かです	*shizuka desu*	It is quiet.
Present Negative	静かじゃないです	*shizuka janai desu*	It is not quiet.
Past Positive	静かでした	*shizuka deshita*	It was quiet.
Past Negative	静かじゃなかったです	*shizuka janakatta desu*	It was not quiet.

2. Using Adverbs

Japanese adverbs describe **how** an action is performed, **to what extent**, or **how often**. They are often derived from adjectives and end in **-く** or **-に**, depending on the type.

Common Adverbs and Their Usage:

Adjective	Adverb	Meaning
早い (*hayai* - fast)	早く (*hayaku*)	Quickly
静か (*shizuka* - quiet)	静かに (*shizuka ni*)	Quietly
簡単 (*kantan* - simple)	簡単に (*kantan ni*)	Simply
よく (*yoku*)	よく (*yoku*)	Often / Well
たくさん (*takusan*)	たくさん (*takusan*)	A lot / Many
少し (*sukoshi*)	少し (*sukoshi*)	A little

Example Sentences:

- 早く走ってください。(*Hayaku hashitte kudasai.*)
  Meaning: Please run quickly.
- 彼は静かに話しました。(*Kare wa shizuka ni hanashimashita.*)
  Meaning: He spoke quietly.

- 日本語をよく勉強します。(*Nihongo o yoku benkyou shimasu.*)
  Meaning: I study Japanese often.

Note: When using adverbs, place them **before the verb** or **adjective** they modify, similar to English.

3. Making Comparisons

To compare objects, people, or situations, Japanese uses the particle より (*yori*) and expressions like もっと (*motto* - more) and 一番 (*ichiban* - the most). Here are a few patterns to help you get started:

Structure	Japanese	Romaji	Meaning
A is more ~ than B	AはBより ˜ です。	*A wa B yori ~ desu.*	A is more ~ than B.
A is the most ~	Aが一番 ˜ です。	*A ga ichiban ~ desu.*	A is the most ~.
A is less ~ than B	AはBほど ˜ ではないです。	*A wa B hodo ~ dewa nai desu.*	A is not as ~ as B.

Example Comparisons:

- 東京は大阪より大きいです。(*Tokyo wa Osaka yori ookii desu.*)
  Meaning: Tokyo is bigger than Osaka.
- この車は一番高いです。(*Kono kuruma wa ichiban takai desu.*)
  Meaning: This car is the most expensive.
- 今日は昨日ほど寒くないです。(*Kyou wa kinou hodo samuku nai desu.*)
  Meaning: Today is not as cold as yesterday.

Practice Tip: Try making comparisons using different adjectives and nouns. For example, compare two cities, two books, or two people using patterns like ˜ より (*yori*) and 一番 (*ichiban*).

Making Comparisons

In Japanese, comparisons are made using the particle より (*yori*) to indicate that one item is more or less of a quality than another. Another common word for comparisons is 一番 (*ichiban*), which means "the most" or "number one." Let's explore these patterns:

1. Using より (*yori*) for "More Than"

- Structure: **AはBより ˜ です**
  (**A wa B yori ~ desu**)
  Meaning: A is more ~ than B.

Example:

- この猫は犬より小さいです。
  (*Kono neko wa inu yori chiisai desu.*)
  Meaning: This cat is smaller than the dog.

2. Using ほど (*hodo*) for "Not as ~ as"

- Structure: **AはBほど˜ ではないです**
  (**A wa B hodo ~ dewa nai desu**)
  Meaning: A is not as ~ as B.

  Example:

  - 東京は大阪ほど寒くないです。
    (*Tokyo wa Osaka hodo samuku nai desu.*)
    Meaning: Tokyo is not as cold as Osaka.

3. Using 一番 (*ichiban*) for "The Most"

- Structure: **Aが一番˜ です**
  (**A ga ichiban ~ desu**)
  Meaning: A is the most ~.

  Example:

  - 彼が一番背が高いです。
    (*Kare ga ichiban se ga takai desu.*)
    Meaning: He is the tallest.

Quick Examples

- 私はコーヒーよりお茶のほうが好きです。
  (*Watashi wa ko-hi- yori ocha no hou ga suki desu.*)
  Meaning: I like tea more than coffee.

- 今日は一番暑いです。
  (*Kyou wa ichiban atsui desu.*)
  Meaning: Today is the hottest.

Key Takeaways

- ❖ **い-adjectives** (e.g., おおきい - big) and **な-adjectives** (e.g., しずかな - quiet) are used to describe nouns with different conjugation rules.

- ❖ **Adverbs** modify verbs, adjectives, or other adverbs and are often formed from adjectives by changing endings (e.g., 早い → 早く - fast → quickly).

- ❖ Use より (*yori*) to express "more than" and ほど (*hodo*) for "not as ~ as."

- ❖ Use 一番 (*ichiban*) to indicate "the most" or "number one."

Exercises

Exercise 1: Fill in the Blanks

Complete the sentences with the correct adjective or adverb form:

1. この部屋はとても＿＿＿＿です。 (This room is very quiet.)

    ○ Options: 静か, 静かに

2. 私の犬は猫より＿＿＿＿です。 (My dog is bigger than the cat.)

    ○ Options: 大きい, 大きく

3. 彼は日本語を＿＿＿＿話します。 (He speaks Japanese well.)

    ○ Options: よい, よく

4. 冬は秋より＿＿＿＿です。 (Winter is colder than autumn.)

    ○ Options: 寒い, 寒く

5. このレストランが＿＿＿＿です。 (This restaurant is the most expensive.)

    ○ Options: 一番高い, 高い

Exercise 2: Translate the Sentences

Translate the following sentences into Japanese:

1. I like sushi more than tempura.
2. This car is the fastest.
3. My house is not as new as yours.
4. Please speak more slowly.
5. That book is more interesting than this one.

Answer Key

Exercise 1: Fill in the Blanks

1. この部屋はとても **静か** です。 (*Kono heya wa totemo shizuka desu.*)
   Meaning: This room is very quiet.

2. 私の犬は猫より **大きい** です。 (*Watashi no inu wa neko yori ookii desu.*)
   Meaning: My dog is bigger than the cat.

3. 彼は日本語を **よく** 話します。 (*Kare wa Nihongo o yoku hanashimasu.*)
   Meaning: He speaks Japanese well.

4. 冬は秋より **寒い** です。 (*Fuyu wa aki yori samui desu.*)
   Meaning: Winter is colder than autumn.

5. このレストランが **一番高い** です。 (*Kono resutoran ga ichiban takai desu.*)
   Meaning: This restaurant is the most expensive.

Exercise 2: Translate the Sentences

1. 私は天ぷらより寿司が好きです。
   (*Watashi wa tenpura yori sushi ga suki desu.*)
   Meaning: I like sushi more than tempura.

2. この車が一番速いです。
   (*Kono kuruma ga ichiban hayai desu.*)
   Meaning: This car is the fastest.

3. 私の家はあなたの家ほど新しくないです。
   (*Watashi no ie wa anata no ie hodo atarashikunai desu.*)
   Meaning: My house is not as new as yours.

4. もっとゆっくり話してください。
   (*Motto yukkuri hanashite kudasai.*)
   Meaning: Please speak more slowly.

5. あの本はこの本より面白いです。
   (*Ano hon wa kono hon yori omoshiroi desu.*)
   Meaning: That book is more interesting than this one.

Conclusion

Congratulations on completing this book! You've gained a strong foundation in Japanese—learning how to introduce yourself, describe objects and situations, navigate conversations, and more. With each chapter, you've built essential skills that will support your continued language-learning journey.

Remember, language mastery comes from consistent practice. Don't hesitate to review and apply what you've learned in real-world scenarios—whether it's chatting with native speakers, watching Japanese media, or practicing on your own.

Keep challenging yourself and expanding your knowledge. With dedication and enthusiasm, fluency is well within reach.

Best of luck on your path to mastering Japanese!

さようなら (Sayounara) — Goodbye, and keep learning!

BOOK 3

Japanese Grammar and Sentence Patterns for Beginners:

Construct Fluent Sentences and Communicate Confidently

Explore to Win

Book Description

Are you struggling to build sentences in Japanese? Do you find it challenging to form grammatically correct sentences and express your thoughts with clarity? If so, you're not alone—but this book is here to help.

"Japanese Grammar and Sentence Patterns for Beginners" is designed to demystify Japanese grammar and provide you with a clear roadmap for constructing fluent sentences. Whether you're a complete beginner or looking to reinforce your foundational knowledge, this book will guide you step-by-step through the core aspects of Japanese grammar, enabling you to communicate more confidently and naturally.

Inside this comprehensive guide, you'll discover:

- **Essential sentence structures and patterns** that form the backbone of Japanese, with easy-to-understand explanations and plenty of examples
- Clear guidance on using **particles**, **nouns**, **verbs**, and **adjectives** to create meaningful sentences
- Practice exercises at the end of each chapter to reinforce your understanding and help solidify your learning
- Strategies for **expressing desires, intentions, and preferences** so you can move beyond basic sentences and start conveying more nuanced ideas
- Tips on **politeness levels and question forms** to ensure that your sentences are both accurate and appropriate for any situation

Each chapter focuses on building your knowledge step-by-step, allowing you to gain a deeper understanding of Japanese sentence patterns and use them naturally. By the end of this book, you'll have the tools to construct clear, precise sentences and communicate confidently in a range of contexts.

Imagine being able to form sentences effortlessly, respond with ease, and express yourself accurately in Japanese. That's what this book aims to achieve. So, if you're ready to transform your Japanese grammar skills and take your language ability to the next level, this guide is for you.

Ready to build a strong grammar foundation and start forming sentences fluently? Grab your copy and begin your journey toward mastering Japanese grammar today!

Introduction

"Grammar is the framework for communication, and without it, words lose their power."
– William Somerset Maugham

When it comes to learning Japanese, mastering grammar can feel overwhelming. Unlike English, Japanese sentence structures, particles, and verb conjugations follow unique rules that often leave beginners unsure of how to combine words to form meaningful sentences. But fear not—this book is here to guide you through the fundamentals and help you gain confidence in constructing fluent sentences.

Whether you're a complete beginner or someone looking to refine your knowledge, **"Japanese Grammar and Sentence Patterns for Beginners"** is designed to make learning grammar straightforward and approachable. We'll break down the complexities of Japanese grammar into simple, digestible steps, allowing you to understand how sentences are formed and why certain rules exist.

The chapters in this book are organized to build upon each other. You'll start by learning the basics of **sentence structure**, including the **subject-object-verb (SOV)** order and how to use **particles** to link words. As you progress, you'll delve into more complex topics like **verb conjugations**, **adjective and adverb usage**, and **expressing desires and intentions**. Each chapter is packed with clear explanations, examples, and exercises to solidify your understanding.

By the end of this book, you will have mastered:

- Constructing sentences with the **correct word order and grammar patterns**
- Effectively using **nouns, verbs, adjectives, and adverbs** to add detail and precision to your statements
- Forming **polite and casual questions**, making comparisons, and linking sentences to express more complex ideas

Remember, learning a language is a journey, and it's okay to go at your own pace. Take time to review, practice, and apply each concept in real-world scenarios. The goal is to not just understand Japanese grammar but to **use it naturally and confidently**.

Happy learning, and がんばって (*ganbatte*)! — Keep going, and good luck!

Chapter 1: Understanding Basic Sentence Structures

"Without grammar, very little can be conveyed; without vocabulary, nothing can be conveyed."
– David Wilkins

When learning a new language, understanding how to build sentences is one of the most critical steps. In Japanese, the sentence structure differs significantly from English, which can sometimes make it feel confusing. However, once you understand the basic patterns, you'll find that Japanese sentence formation is surprisingly logical and systematic.

This chapter will introduce you to the **SOV (Subject-Object-Verb)** order, which forms the foundation of Japanese sentences. You'll also learn about the essential role **particles** play in linking words and providing meaning. By mastering these core elements, you can construct simple yet meaningful sentences and develop a solid understanding of Japanese grammar.

We'll start by breaking down the SOV pattern, understanding how subjects and objects are arranged, and how verbs always come at the end. Then, we'll look at how different **particles** like は (*wa*), を (*wo*), and が (*ga*) are used to mark subjects, objects, and other sentence components, making your sentences clear and coherent.

Let's dive in and start building your sentence structure foundation!

The SOV Order in Japanese

Unlike English, where sentences follow a **subject-verb-object (SVO)** pattern (e.g., "I eat sushi"), Japanese follows a **subject-object-verb (SOV)** structure. This means that the **verb** always comes **at the end** of the sentence. Understanding this order is crucial to constructing sentences correctly.

Basic SOV Pattern:

1. **Subject → Object → Verb**

Example:

- 私はすしを食べます。 (*Watashi wa sushi o tabemasu.*)
    - **Breakdown**:
        - **Subject**: 私 (*watashi*) – I
        - **Object**: すし (*sushi*) – sushi
        - **Verb**: 食べます (*tabemasu*) – eat
    - **Meaning**: I eat sushi.

In Japanese, **the verb is always placed at the end**, regardless of how many elements are in the sentence. The subject can be omitted if it's clear from the context.

Key Points to Remember:

- The **subject** and **object** often appear at the beginning, but the **verb** always ends the sentence.
- Japanese uses **particles** to clarify the role of each word in a sentence. Let's explore this next.

Using Particles for Sentence Clarity

In Japanese, **particles** are small words placed after nouns, pronouns, and phrases to indicate the grammatical role of each word in a sentence.

Think of them as **markers** that define the **function** of a word, such as the subject, object, or direction.

Here's an overview of some key particles and their roles:

1. は (*wa*) – Topic Marker

- Marks the **topic** of the sentence (often the subject)
- Indicates what the sentence is **about**

Example:

- 私は学生です。 (*Watashi wa gakusei desu.*)
  - **Meaning**: I am a student.
  - **Function**: は (*wa*) marks "私" (*watashi* - I) as the topic.

2. が (*ga*) – Subject Marker

- Emphasizes or introduces the **subject**
- Used when the subject is **new information** or in **question sentences**

Example:

- 誰が来ますか？ (*Dare ga kimasu ka?*)
  - **Meaning**: Who is coming?
  - **Function**: が (*ga*) marks "誰" (*dare* - who) as the subject.

3. を (*wo*) – Direct Object Marker

- Marks the **direct object** of an action

Example:

- すしを食べます。 (*Sushi o tabemasu.*)
  - **Meaning**: I eat sushi.
  - **Function**: を (*wo*) marks "すし" (*sushi*) as the direct object being eaten.

4. に (*ni*) and へ (*e*) – Direction/Location Markers

- に (*ni*) indicates the **specific destination**, time, or direction.
- へ (*e*) also marks **direction** but with less specificity.

Examples:

- 学校に行きます。 (*Gakkou ni ikimasu.*)
  - **Meaning**: I go to school.
- 家へ帰ります。 (*Ie e kaerimasu.*)
  - **Meaning**: I return home.

5. で (*de*) – Location or Means Marker

- Indicates the **location** of an action or the **means** by which an action is performed

Example:

- 図書館で本を読みます。 (*Toshokan de hon o yomimasu.*)
  - **Meaning**: I read a book at the library.
  - **Function**: で (*de*) marks the **location** "図書館" (*toshokan* - library).

Using Particles Together:

In longer sentences, multiple particles are combined to show more complex structures:

- 私は毎日バスで学校に行きます。 (*Watashi wa mainichi basu de gakkou ni ikimasu.*)
  - **Meaning**: I go to school by bus every day.
  - **Particles Used**:
    - は (*wa*) marks "私" (*watashi*) as the topic.
    - で (*de*) indicates "バス" (*basu*) as the means of transportation.
    - に (*ni*) marks "学校" (*gakkou*) as the destination.

Understanding how these particles interact is key to making your sentences clear and accurate.

Key Takeaways

- ❖ **Japanese follows an SOV (Subject-Object-Verb) sentence structure**, meaning the verb always comes at the end.
- ❖ **Particles** define the role of words in a sentence:
  - ➢ は (*wa*): Marks the **topic**
  - ➢ が (*ga*): Highlights the **subject**
  - ➢ を (*wo*): Indicates the **direct object**
  - ➢ に (*ni*) and へ (*e*): Show **direction** or **destination**
  - ➢ で (*de*): Denotes the **location** or **means** of an action
- ❖ Using the correct particle is crucial for creating clear and meaningful sentences in Japanese.

Exercises

Exercise 1: Identifying Sentence Structure
Label the components of the following sentence as **Subject (S)**, **Object (O)**, or **Verb (V)**:

1. 私はりんごを食べます。(*Watashi wa ringo o tabemasu.*)
2. 猫が魚を見ます。(*Neko ga sakana o mimasu.*)
3. 田中さんは図書館で勉強します。(*Tanaka-san wa toshokan de benkyou shimasu.*)

Exercise 2: Fill in the Missing Particles
Choose the correct particle to complete each sentence:

1. 私＿＿＿すし＿＿＿食べます。
   Options: は, が, を
2. 彼＿＿＿車＿＿＿運転します。
   Options: が, で, を
3. 母は家＿＿＿料理をします。
   Options: に, で, へ
4. 友達＿＿＿学校＿＿＿来ます。
   Options: に, が, へ
5. 私は公園＿＿＿走ります。
   Options: で, に, を

Exercise 3: Sentence Translation
Translate the following sentences into Japanese using the correct particles:

1. I read a book at the library.
2. The dog drinks water.
3. She goes to the office by train.
4. I study Japanese every day.
5. He writes a letter to his friend.

Answer Key

Exercise 1: Identifying Sentence Structure

1. 私はりんごを食べます。(*Watashi wa ringo o tabemasu.*)
   - **Subject**: 私 (*watashi*) – I
   - **Object**: りんご (*ringo*) – apple
   - **Verb**: 食べます (*tabemasu*) – eat

2. 猫が魚を見ます。(*Neko ga sakana o mimasu.*)
   - **Subject**: 猫 (*neko*) – cat
   - **Object**: 魚 (*sakana*) – fish
   - **Verb**: 見ます (*mimasu*) – see

3. 田中さんは図書館で勉強します。(*Tanaka-san wa toshokan de benkyou shimasu.*)
   - **Subject**: 田中さん (*Tanaka-san*) – Mr./Ms. Tanaka
   - **Location**: 図書館で (*toshokan de*) – at the library
   - **Verb**: 勉強します (*benkyou shimasu*) – study

Exercise 2: Fill in the Missing Particles

1. 私 **は** **すし** **を** 食べます。
   (*Watashi wa sushi o tabemasu.*)
   Meaning: I eat sushi.

2. 彼 **が** 車 **を** 運転します。
   (*Kare ga kuruma o untenshimasu.*)
   Meaning: He drives a car.

3. 母は家 **で** 料理をします。
   (*Haha wa ie de ryouri o shimasu.*)
   Meaning: My mother cooks at home.

4. 友達 **が** 学校 **に** 来ます。
   (*Tomodachi ga gakkou ni kimasu.*)
   Meaning: My friend comes to school.

5. 私は公園 **で** 走ります。
   (*Watashi wa kouen de hashirimasu.*)
   Meaning: I run at the park.

Exercise 3: Sentence Translation

1. I read a book at the library.
    - 図書館で本を読みます。
      (*Toshokan de hon o yomimasu.*)
2. The dog drinks water.
    - 犬が水を飲みます。
      (*Inu ga mizu o nomimasu.*)
3. She goes to the office by train.
    - 彼女は電車で会社に行きます。
      (*Kanojo wa densha de kaisha ni ikimasu.*)
4. I study Japanese every day.
    - 私は毎日日本語を勉強します。
      (*Watashi wa mainichi nihongo o benkyou shimasu.*)
5. He writes a letter to his friend.
    - 彼は友達に手紙を書きます。
      (*Kare wa tomodachi ni tegami o kakimasu.*)

Chapter 2: Nouns, Pronouns, and Articles

"Words are, of course, the most powerful drug used by mankind."

– Rudyard Kipling

Nouns and pronouns are essential building blocks of any language, and Japanese is no different. However, unlike English, Japanese does not use **articles** (like "a," "an," or "the"), and it handles **gender and numbers** differently. This can be both a relief and a challenge for learners.

In this chapter, we'll dive into the structure and usage of **nouns** and **pronouns** in Japanese. You'll learn how to identify and use **gender-neutral nouns**, refer to **people and objects** correctly, and express **numbers** (singular vs. plural) without needing extra words. We'll also explore how to create sentences that appropriately reflect the **agreement** between nouns and pronouns.

By the end of this chapter, you'll be able to:

1. Use **Japanese nouns** to describe people, places, and things accurately.
2. Understand how **pronouns** work and how to choose the right one for the context.
3. Create sentences that clearly indicate the **number and agreement** without confusion.

Let's begin by understanding how **gender** and **number** are expressed in Japanese!

Gender and Number in Japanese

Unlike many Western languages, Japanese does not use **gendered nouns** or **articles** to differentiate between male and female or singular and plural forms. This can simplify sentence construction, but it also requires a different approach to understanding context.

1. Gender in Japanese Nouns

Japanese nouns are inherently **gender-neutral**. Words like "teacher," "student," or "friend" do not change based on the gender of the person:

- 先生 (*sensei*) – Teacher
- 学生 (*gakusei*) – Student
- 友達 (*tomodachi*) – Friend

To specify gender, additional words such as 男の～ (*otoko no ~*) for "male" or 女の～ (*onna no ~*) for "female" are sometimes added:

- 男の学生 (*otoko no gakusei*) – Male student
- 女の友達 (*onna no tomodachi*) – Female friend

However, these distinctions are used sparingly. In most cases, the context of the conversation will indicate the gender if it's relevant.

2. Number in Japanese Nouns

Japanese does not typically use separate plural forms. The same noun can indicate **singular** or **plural** depending on the context:

- 猫 (*neko*) – Cat / Cats
- 本 (*hon*) – Book / Books

To make a noun explicitly plural, the suffix ˜たち (*-tachi*) is sometimes used, particularly with **people**:

- 子供たち (*kodomo-tachi*) – Children
- 彼ら (*karera*) – They (male or mixed group)
- 彼女たち (*kanojotachi*) – They (female group)

But for most inanimate objects, simply using the noun with a context word or numeral is enough:

- 三冊の本 (*san-satsu no hon*) – Three books
- 多くの猫 (*ooku no neko*) – Many cats

3. Expressing Quantity and Number

To express **quantity**, Japanese relies on **numerals** and **counters**. Counters are specific words used to count different categories of objects, like books, animals, or people:

Type of Object	Counter	Example
Small objects	˜つ (*-tsu*)	三つ (*mittsu*) – Three (small items)
People	˜人 (*-nin*)	二人 (*futari*) – Two people
Books	˜冊 (*-satsu*)	四冊 (*yon-satsu*) –Four books
Flat objects	˜枚 (*-mai*)	五枚 (*go-mai*) – Five sheets
Animals	˜匹 (*-hiki*)	六匹 (*roppiki*) – Six animals

Example Sentences:

- 本が三冊あります。 (*Hon ga san-satsu arimasu.*)
  Meaning: There are three books.

- 猫が二匹います。 (*Neko ga ni-hiki imasu.*)
  Meaning: There are two cats.

By using context, counters, and numerals, you can clearly indicate whether a noun is singular or plural, even without changing the noun itself.

Creating Sentences with Proper Agreement

In Japanese, constructing sentences with the proper **agreement** is different from English because nouns do not change to reflect **number** or **gender**. Instead, proper agreement is achieved through **particles**, **context**, and using correct **pronouns** or **counters**.

1. Matching Pronouns and Nouns

Japanese pronouns are also **gender-neutral** and often omitted unless needed for clarity. When used, pronouns should match the **number** and **person** you're referring to:

- 私 (*watashi*) – I / Me
- あなた (*anata*) – You
- 彼 (*kare*) – He / Him
- 彼女 (*kanojo*) – She / Her
- 私たち (*watashi-tachi*) – We / Us
- 彼ら (*karera*) – They (male or mixed group)
- 彼女たち (*kanojotachi*) – They (female group)

Example Sentences:

- 私は学生です。 (*Watashi wa gakusei desu.*)
  Meaning: I am a student.
- 彼らは先生です。 (*Karera wa sensei desu.*)
  Meaning: They are teachers.

2. Ensuring Agreement with Counters

When referring to quantities or plural forms, use **counters** along with the noun to clarify the number of items. This makes your sentences precise and avoids confusion.

Examples:

- 猫が三匹います。 (*Neko ga san-biki imasu.*)
  Meaning: There are three cats.
  - 猫 (*neko*): Cat
  - 三匹 (*san-biki*): Three (small animals)

- 学生が五人います。(*Gakusei ga go-nin imasu.*)
  Meaning: There are five students.
  - 学生 (*gakusei*): Student
  - 五人 (*go-nin*): Five (people)

Using counters appropriately ensures that the quantity is clear, even when the noun itself does not change.

3. Expressing Ownership and Possession

In Japanese, possession is shown using the particle の (*no*) between the owner and the object:

- **AのB** = A's B / B belonging to A
  - 私の本 (*watashi no hon*) – My book
  - 彼の犬 (*kare no inu*) – His dog

This structure does not change based on number or gender, making agreement simpler. Use の (*no*) to connect the noun or pronoun to show who owns what:

Example Sentences:

- これは私の車です。(*Kore wa watashi no kuruma desu.*)
  Meaning: This is my car.
- 彼女の名前は花子です。(*Kanojo no namae wa Hanako desu.*)
  Meaning: Her name is Hanako.

4. Agreement with Descriptive Adjectives

When using **adjectives** to describe nouns, ensure that the adjective is in the **correct form** to match the noun. In Japanese, adjectives do not change based on number or gender, but their endings may change depending on tense or negation:

Example:

- 小さい犬 (*chiisai inu*) – A small dog
- 大きい猫 (*ookii neko*) – A big cat

Agreement Example:

- その本は面白いです。(*Sono hon wa omoshiroi desu.*)
  Meaning: That book is interesting.
- この映画は長いです。(*Kono eiga wa nagai desu.*)
  Meaning: This movie is long.

In each example, the adjective **agrees** with the noun it describes but does not change form based on the noun's gender or number.

Key Takeaways

❖ Japanese nouns and pronouns are **gender-neutral** and rarely change for **number** (singular/plural).

❖ To specify plural forms, use suffixes like 〜たち (-*tachi*) for people or rely on **counters** for clarity.

❖ **Pronouns** such as 私 (*watashi*) and 彼 (*kare*) do not have gender-specific endings but change depending on context.

❖ Use **particles** like の (*no*) for possession (e.g., 私の本 - *watashi no hon* - my book).

❖ Adjectives remain the same regardless of the gender or number of the noun they describe, simplifying agreement.

Exercises

Exercise 1: Fill in the Missing Pronoun

Choose the correct pronoun to complete each sentence:

1. ＿＿＿＿ は学生です。 (I am a student.)
   - Options: 彼, 私, あなた
2. ＿＿＿＿ の名前は田中です。 (Her name is Tanaka.)
   - Options: 彼女, 彼, 私
3. ＿＿＿＿ は友達です。 (They are friends.)
   - Options: 彼ら, 私たち, 彼
4. ＿＿＿＿ はどこですか？ (Where is your book?)
   - Options: あなた, あなたの, 彼の
5. ＿＿＿＿ は料理が上手です。 (He is good at cooking.)
   - Options: 彼女, 私, 彼

Exercise 2: Translate the Sentences

Translate the following sentences into Japanese:

1. This is my car.
2. I am from America.
3. She is a teacher.
4. They are Japanese students.
5. My friend's dog is big.

Answer Key

Exercise 1: Fill in the Missing Pronoun

1. 私 は学生です。(*Watashi wa gakusei desu.*)

   ○ **Meaning**: I am a student.

2. 彼女 の名前は田中です。(*Kanojo no namae wa Tanaka desu.*)

   ○ **Meaning**: Her name is Tanaka.

3. 彼ら は友達です。(*Karera wa tomodachi desu.*)

   ○ **Meaning**: They are friends.

4. **あなたの** 本はどこですか？(*Anata no hon wa doko desu ka?*)

   ○ **Meaning**: Where is your book?

5. 彼 は料理が上手です。(*Kare wa ryouri ga jouzu desu.*)

   ○ **Meaning**: He is good at cooking.

Exercise 2: Translate the Sentences

1. これは私の車です。
   (*Kore wa watashi no kuruma desu.*)
   Meaning: This is my car.

2. 私はアメリカ出身です。
   (*Watashi wa Amerika shusshin desu.*)
   Meaning: I am from America.

3. 彼女は先生です。
   (*Kanojo wa sensei desu.*)
   Meaning: She is a teacher.

4. 彼らは日本人の学生です。
   (*Karera wa Nihonjin no gakusei desu.*)
   Meaning: They are Japanese students.

5. 私の友達の犬は大きいです。
   (*Watashi no tomodachi no inu wa ookii desu.*)
   Meaning: My friend's dog is big.

Chapter 3: Mastering Verb Forms

"Actions speak louder than words, but words become actions through verbs."
– Unknown

Verbs are the foundation of communication in Japanese. They define actions, states of being, and the flow of time within a sentence. Unlike English, Japanese verbs follow a structured set of rules for **conjugation**, making them predictable once you understand the basic patterns. Mastering these forms is essential to expressing yourself accurately and clearly.

In this chapter, we'll explore the essentials of **verb conjugation**, starting with an introduction to **verb groups** and the different ways verbs change depending on **tense** and **affirmation**. You'll learn how to:

1. Differentiate between **う-Verbs**, **る-Verbs**, and **Irregular Verbs**.
2. Form the **affirmative** and **negative** versions of each verb.
3. Conjugate verbs into the **present**, **past**, and **future** tenses to describe actions at different time points.

By the end of this chapter, you'll be able to apply these rules to construct meaningful sentences, giving your Japanese a solid grammatical foundation.

Introduction to Verb Conjugation

In Japanese, verbs are divided into three main groups based on their conjugation patterns: **う-Verbs**, **る-Verbs**, and **Irregular Verbs**.

Learning to identify which group a verb belongs to is the first step to mastering how to conjugate them correctly in various tenses.

Each group follows a unique set of rules, but forming sentences becomes much easier once these patterns are learned.

1. Verb Groups Overview

1. **う-Verbs (Group 1 Verbs)**
   - Also called **Godan Verbs**
   - Typically end in **-u** sounds, such as う, く, す, つ, む, ぶ, る, or ぐ
   - Example Verbs:
     - 書く (*kaku*) – To write
     - 話す (*hanasu*) – To speak

- ■ 泳ぐ (*oyogu*) – To swim

2. **る-Verbs (Group 2 Verbs)**
   - ○ Also called **Ichidan Verbs**
   - ○ End in **-iru** or **-eru** sounds
   - ○ Example Verbs:
     - ■ 食べる (*taberu*) – To eat
     - ■ 見る (*miru*) – To see
     - ■ 起きる (*okiru*) – To wake up

3. **Irregular Verbs (Group 3 Verbs)**
   - ○ Only a few verbs fall into this category, but they are frequently used and have unique conjugation patterns.
   - ○ Most common examples:
     - ■ する (*suru*) – To do
     - ■ 来る (*kuru*) – To come

2. Identifying Verb Groups

To determine which group a verb belongs to, look at its **dictionary form** (the base form of the verb). Here's a simple rule:

- **If a verb ends in る** and is preceded by an **i or e sound** (such as *miru* or *taberu*), it is usually a **る-Verb**.
- **If a verb ends in る** but is preceded by an **a, u, or o sound** (like *kaeru*), or ends in other -u sounds (e.g., *kiku*), it is typically an **う-Verb**.
- する (*suru*) and 来る (*kuru*) are exceptions and belong to the **Irregular Verbs** group.

3. Conjugation Basics: The Root Form

Before learning tense changes, it's essential to identify the **root form** of the verb. The root is the unchanged part of the verb that remains constant throughout conjugation:

Verb Group	Dictionary Form	Root Form	Example
う-Verbs	書く (*kaku*)	書 (*ka*)	書く → 書かない (*kaku → kakanai*)
る-Verbs	食べる (*taberu*)	食べ (*tabe*)	食べる → 食べない (*taberu → tabenai*)
Irregular	する (*suru*)	し (*shi*)	する → しない (*suru → shinai*)

Understanding these root forms will help when applying tense and affirmative/negative transformations, which we'll explore next.

The Present, Past, and Future Tense

Japanese verb tenses are more straightforward compared to English. Japanese uses two basic tenses: **Past** and **Non-Past**. The Non-Past form can refer to both the present and future, depending on the context. The meaning of future actions is often derived from time expressions (e.g., 明日 'ashita' for 'tomorrow').

Let's break down the **affirmative** and **negative** conjugations for each tense, focusing on う-Verbs, る-Verbs, and **Irregular Verbs**.

1. Present/Non-Past Tense

- Indicates actions that are happening **now** or **habitually** (e.g., "I eat sushi") or will occur in the **future** (e.g., "I will eat sushi").
- The dictionary form of the verb is usually used for **casual** affirmative statements. For **polite** speech, attach -ます (-masu) to the verb root.

Verb Group	Affirmative	Negative
う-Verbs	書く (*kaku*) – To write	書かない (*kakanai*) – To not write
る-Verbs	食べる (*taberu*) – To eat	食べない (*tabenai*) – To not eat
Irregular	する (*suru*) – To do / 来る (*kuru*) – To come	しない (*shinai*) – To not do / 来ない (*konai*) – To not come

Polite Present/Non-Past Form:

- 書きます (*kakimasu*) – I write
- 食べます (*tabemasu*) – I eat
- しません (*shimasen*) – I do not do
- 来ます (*kimasu*) – I come

2. Past Tense

- Describes actions that **happened** in the past.
- The past tense for **affirmative** is formed by modifying the verb stem, and for **negative**, by changing the -ない (-*nai*) form to -なかった (-*nakatta*).

Verb Group	Affirmative	Negative
う -Verbs	書いた (*kaita*) – Wrote	書かなかった (*kakanakatta*) – Did not write
る -Verbs	食べた (*tabeta*) – Ate	食べなかった (*tabenakatta*) – Did not eat
Irregular	した (*shita*) – Did / 来た (*kita*) – Came	しなかった (*shinakatta*) – Did not do / 来なかった (*konakatta*) – Did not come

Polite Past Form:

- 書きました (*kakimashita*) – I wrote
- 食べました (*tabemashita*) – I ate
- しませんでした (*shimasen deshita*) – I did not do
- 来ました (*kimashita*) – I came

3. Future Tense

Japanese does not have a specific **future tense**. The **Non-Past** form is used to indicate future actions based on context:

Examples:

- 彼は明日来ます。 (*Kare wa ashita kimasu.*)
  Meaning: He **will come** tomorrow.
- 私は寿司を食べます。 (*Watashi wa sushi o tabemasu.*)
  Meaning: I **will eat** sushi.

To make the future more explicit, you can add time markers like 明日 (*ashita* - tomorrow), 来週 (*raishuu* - next week), or 今度 (*kondo* - next time).

Summary of Conjugation Patterns

Tense	う-Verbs	る-Verbs	Irregular Verbs
Present Affirmative	書く (*kaku*)	食べる (*taberu*)	する (*suru*), 来る (*kuru*)
Present Negative	書かない (*kakanai*)	食べない (*tabenai*)	しない (*shinai*), 来ない (*konai*)
Past Affirmative	書いた (*kaita*)	食べた (*tabeta*)	した (*shita*), 来た (*kita*)
Past Negative	書かなかった (*kakanakatta*)	食べなかった (*tabenakatta*)	しなかった (*shinakatta*), 来なかった (*konakatta*)

By learning these core patterns, you'll be able to express actions in any timeframe with ease.

Key Takeaways

❖ Japanese verbs are categorized into **three groups**: **う-Verbs**, **る-Verbs**, and **Irregular Verbs**, each with distinct conjugation patterns.

❖ Japanese uses only two basic tenses, **Past** and **Non-Past**, which cover both the **present** and **future**.

❖ **Present/Non-Past Affirmative** is the base form (e.g., 書く for "write"), and the **Present/Non-Past Negative** is formed by adding **-ない** (e.g., 書かない for "do not write").

❖ **Past Affirmative** forms often end in **-た** (e.g., 書いた for "wrote"), while the **Past Negative** ends in **-なかった** (e.g., 書かなかった for "did not write").

❖ Irregular verbs like **する** (*suru* - to do) and **来る** (*kuru* - to come) follow unique conjugation rules and need to be memorized.

Exercises

Exercise 1: Verb Conjugation Practice

Conjugate the following verbs into the **Present Affirmative**, **Present Negative**, **Past Affirmative**, and **Past Negative** forms:

1. 読む (*yomu*) – To read
2. 見る (*miru*) – To see
3. する (*suru*) – To do
4. 話す (*hanasu*) – To speak
5. 来る (*kuru*) – To come

Exercise 2: Sentence Completion

Complete the sentences using the correct verb form:

1. 私は本を＿＿＿＿＿。 (*watashi wa hon o ＿＿＿＿＿.*)
   Meaning: I read books.
   - Options: 読む, 読みます, 読まない
2. 彼は昨日テレビを＿＿＿＿＿。 (*kare wa kinou terebi o ＿＿＿＿＿.*)
   Meaning: He watched TV yesterday.
   - Options: 見る, 見た, 見ない
3. 私たちは来週、京都に＿＿＿＿＿。 (*watashitachi wa raishuu, Kyoto ni ＿＿＿＿＿.*)
   Meaning: We will go to Kyoto next week.
   - Options: 行きます, 行った, 行かない
4. 彼女は掃除を＿＿＿＿＿。 (*kanojo wa souji o ＿＿＿＿＿.*)
   Meaning: She does not clean.
   - Options: しない, します, しなかった
5. 子供たちは公園で＿＿＿＿＿。 (*kodomotachi wa kouen de ＿＿＿＿＿.*)
   Meaning: The children played at the park.
   - Options: 遊んだ, 遊ぶ, 遊ばない

Exercise 3: Translation Practice

Translate the following sentences into Japanese:

1. I will eat sushi tomorrow.
2. They did not go to school.
3. My friend comes to my house every week.
4. I did not do my homework.
5. She speaks Japanese well.

Answer Key

Exercise 1: Verb Conjugation Practice

1. 読む (*yomu*) – To read

   - Present Affirmative: 読む (*yomu*)
   - Present Negative: 読まない (*yomanai*)
   - Past Affirmative: 読んだ (*yonda*)
   - Past Negative: 読まなかった (*yomanakatta*)

2. 見る (*miru*) – To see

   - Present Affirmative: 見る (*miru*)
   - Present Negative: 見ない (*minai*)
   - Past Affirmative: 見た (*mita*)
   - Past Negative: 見なかった (*minakatta*)

3. する (*suru*) – To do

   - Present Affirmative: する (*suru*)
   - Present Negative: しない (*shinai*)
   - Past Affirmative: した (*shita*)
   - Past Negative: しなかった (*shinakatta*)

4. 話す (*hanasu*) – To speak

   - Present Affirmative: 話す (*hanasu*)
   - Present Negative: 話さない (*hanasanai*)
   - Past Affirmative: 話した (*hanashita*)
   - Past Negative: 話さなかった (*hanasanakatta*)

5. 来る (*kuru*) – To come

   - Present Affirmative: 来る (*kuru*)
   - Present Negative: 来ない (*konai*)
   - Past Affirmative: 来た (*kita*)
   - Past Negative: 来なかった (*konakatta*)

Exercise 2: Sentence Completion

1. 私は本を読みます。 (*Watashi wa hon o yomimasu.*)
   Meaning: I read books.

2. 彼は昨日テレビを見た。 (*Kare wa kinou terebi o mita.*)
   Meaning: He watched TV yesterday.

3. 私たちは来週、京都に行きます。 (*Watashitachi wa raishuu, Kyoto ni ikimasu.*)
   Meaning: We will go to Kyoto next week.

4. 彼女は掃除をしない。 (*Kanojo wa souji o shinai.*)
   Meaning: She does not clean.

5. 子供たちは公園で遊んだ。 (*Kodomotachi wa kouen de asonda.*)
   Meaning: The children played at the park.

Exercise 3: Translation Practice

1. I will eat sushi tomorrow.
   - 私は明日寿司を食べます。
     (*Watashi wa ashita sushi o tabemasu.*)

2. They did not go to school.
   - 彼らは学校に行きませんでした。
     (*Karera wa gakkou ni ikimasen deshita.*)

3. My friend comes to my house every week.
   - 私の友達は毎週私の家に来ます。
     (*Watashi no tomodachi wa maishuu watashi no ie ni kimasu.*)

4. I did not do my homework.
   - 私は宿題をしませんでした。
     (*Watashi wa shukudai o shimasen deshita.*)

5. She speaks Japanese well.
   - 彼女は日本語を上手に話します。
     (*Kanojo wa Nihongo o jouzu ni hanashimasu.*)

Chapter 4: The Use of Adjectives and Adverbs

"Adjectives are the fine threads that bring color to language, while adverbs weave rhythm into every sentence."
– Unknown

In Japanese, adjectives and adverbs are powerful tools that allow you to describe people, objects, and actions more vividly. They add depth to your language, helping you express *what* something is and *how* it is. Understanding how to use them correctly will enable you to communicate more naturally and fluently.

In this chapter, we'll explore:

1. **Adjective Placement and Agreement**: Learn how to place adjectives properly in sentences and understand how they interact with nouns.
2. **Using Adverbs to Modify Actions**: Discover how to form adverbs from adjectives and use them to describe verbs, adjectives, and even other adverbs.

By the end of this chapter, you'll be able to create more descriptive sentences, express nuances, and talk about events and actions with greater clarity and impact.

Ready to dive into the art of **Japanese adjectives and adverbs**? Let's get started with **Adjective Placement and Agreement**!

Adjective Placement and Agreement

In Japanese, adjectives are used to describe **nouns** and can either be placed **before the noun** (attributive use) or **at the end of a sentence** (predicate use). Understanding these two placements is essential for constructing clear and accurate sentences.

1. Types of Adjectives

Japanese adjectives are classified into two main types:

1. **い-Adjectives (i-adjectives)**
   - End in **-い** (e.g., 高い - *takai* - high/tall)
   - Can be placed before a noun or used as the predicate
2. **Examples**:
   - 高いビル (*takai biru*) – A tall building
   - このビルは高いです。(*Kono biru wa takai desu.*) – This building is tall.

3. **な-Adjectives (na-adjectives)**
   - End with **な** when directly modifying a noun (e.g., **静かな** - *shizukana* - quiet).
   - **な**-adjectives use 'です' or nothing in predicate use, depending on formality.
4. **Examples**:
   - 静かな部屋 (*shizukana heya*) – A quiet room
   - 部屋は静かです。(*Heya wa shizuka desu.*) – The room is quiet.

2. Adjective Agreement

Unlike English, Japanese adjectives do not change based on **number** or **gender**. However, they **conjugate** to express **tense** and **negation**:

Form	**い-Adjective Example**	**な-Adjective Example**
Present Affirmative	高い (*takai*) – Is tall	静かです (*shizuka desu*) – Is quiet
Present Negative	高くない (*takakunai*) – Not tall	静かじゃない (*shizuka janai*) – Not quiet
Past Affirmative	高かった (*takakatta*) – Was tall	静かでした (*shizuka deshita*) – Was quiet
Past Negative	高くなかった (*takakunakatta*) – Was not tall	静かじゃなかった (*shizuka janakatta*) – Was not quiet

Now that we've covered adjectives, let's explore how to use **adverbs** to modify actions in the next section!

Using Adverbs to Modify Actions

Adverbs in Japanese modify **verbs**, **adjectives**, or even other adverbs, describing *how, when, where,* or *to what extent* an action is performed. Most adverbs are either standalone words or are formed by changing the ending of **い-adjectives** and **な-adjectives**.

1. Forming Adverbs

- **い-Adjectives**: Replace **い** with **く**.

- ○ Example:
    - 速い (*hayai*) – Fast → 速く (*hayaku*) – Quickly
    - 面白い (*omoshiroi*) – Interesting → 面白く (*omoshiroku*) – Interestingly
- **な-Adjectives**: Replace **な** with **に**.
  - ○ Example:
    - 簡単な (*kantan-na*) – Simple → 簡単に (*kantan-ni*) – Simply
    - 静かな (*shizuka-na*) – Quiet → 静かに (*shizuka-ni*) – Quietly

2. Using Adverbs in Sentences

Adverbs are usually placed **before the verb** or **adjective** they modify:

- 彼は速く走ります。 (*Kare wa hayaku hashirimasu.*)
  Meaning: He runs quickly.
- 彼女は静かに話します。 (*Kanojo wa shizuka ni hanashimasu.*)
  Meaning: She speaks quietly.

By incorporating adverbs, you add detail and nuance to your sentences, making your speech more expressive.

Key Takeaways

- ❖ **い-Adjectives** end in **-い** (e.g., 高い - tall), and **な-Adjectives** use **-な** when directly modifying a noun (e.g., 静かな - quiet).

- ❖ Adjectives can be used to describe nouns or as predicates at the end of a sentence.

- ❖ To form **adverbs**, change the ending **い** to **く** (e.g., 速い → 速く - fast → quickly) or **な** to **に** (e.g., 簡単な → 簡単に - simple → simply).

- ❖ Adverbs are usually placed **before the verb** or **adjective** they modify.

Exercises

Exercise 1: Adjective and Adverb Conjugation

Convert the given adjectives into the specified form:

1. 高い (*takai* - tall) → Past Affirmative

2. 便利な (*benrina* - convenient) → Present Negative

3. 速い (*hayai* - fast) → Adverb

4. 簡単な (*kantan-na* - simple) → Adverb

5. 美しい (*utsukushii* - beautiful) → Present Negative

Exercise 2: Sentence Completion

Complete the sentences using the correct form of the adjective or adverb:

1. この本は＿＿＿＿です。(*kono hon wa ＿＿＿＿ desu.*)

   ○ Options: 面白い, 面白く, 面白くない
   Meaning: This book is interesting.

2. 彼は＿＿＿＿歌います。(*kare wa ＿＿＿＿ utaimasu.*)

   ○ Options: 上手に, 上手な, 上手く
   Meaning: He sings well.

3. この部屋は＿＿＿＿。(*kono heya wa ＿＿＿＿.*)

   ○ Options: 静かです, 静かに, 静かな
   Meaning: This room is quiet.

4. 彼女は＿＿＿＿話しました。(*kanojo wa ＿＿＿＿ hanashimashita.*)

   ○ Options: 速い, 速く, 速かった
   Meaning: She spoke quickly.

5. この映画は＿＿＿＿です。(*kono eiga wa ＿＿＿＿ desu.*)

   ○ Options: 短く, 短い, 短くない
   Meaning: This movie is short.

Exercise 3: Translation Practice

Translate the following sentences into Japanese:

1. This is a beautiful flower.

2. He runs fast.

3. My house is not big.

4. She spoke simply.

5. This book is not interesting.

Answer Key

Exercise 1: Adjective and Adverb Conjugation

1. 高い (*takai*) → 高かった (*takakatta*)
   - Past Affirmative: Was tall.
2. 便利な (*benrina*) → 便利じゃない (*benri janai*)
   - Present Negative: Not convenient.
3. 速い (*hayai*) → 速く (*hayaku*)
   - Adverb: Quickly.
4. 簡単な (*kantan-na*) → 簡単に (*kantan-ni*)
   - Adverb: Simply.
5. 美しい (*utsukushii*) → 美しくない (*utsukushikunai*)
   - Present Negative: Not beautiful.

Exercise 2: Sentence Completion

1. この本は面白いです。 (*Kono hon wa omoshiroi desu.*)
   Meaning: This book is interesting.
2. 彼は上手に歌います。 (*Kare wa jouzu ni utaimasu.*)
   Meaning: He sings well.
3. この部屋は静かです。 (*Kono heya wa shizuka desu.*)
   Meaning: This room is quiet.
4. 彼女は速く話しました。 (*Kanojo wa hayaku hanashimashita.*)
   Meaning: She spoke quickly.
5. この映画は短いです。 (*Kono eiga wa mijikai desu.*)
   Meaning: This movie is short.

Exercise 3: Translation Practice

1. This is a beautiful flower.
   - これは美しい花です。
     (*Kore wa utsukushii hana desu.*)
2. He runs fast.
   - 彼は速く走ります。
     (*Kare wa hayaku hashirimasu.*)
3. My house is not big.
   - 私の家は大きくないです。
     (*Watashi no ie wa ookikunai desu.*)

4. She spoke simply.
    - 彼女は簡単に話しました。
      (*Kanojo wa kantan ni hanashimashita.*)
5. This book is not interesting.
    - この本は面白くないです。
      (*Kono hon wa omoshirokunai desu.*)

Chapter 5: Expressing Desires and Intentions

"Desire is the starting point of all achievement."
– Napoleon Hill

Being able to express your desires and intentions is an important step in mastering any language. In Japanese, expressing **wants** and **intentions** requires specific verb forms and patterns that differ from basic conjugation rules. Learning these structures will enable you to talk about what you *want to do*, *plan to do*, or *intend to do*—a crucial skill for everyday conversations.

In this chapter, we'll explore:

1. The **"Want to" Form**: Learn how to use たい (*-tai*) to express what you want to do.

2. The **"Plan to"** and **"Intend to" Patterns**: Discover how to use patterns like つもりです (*tsumori desu*) and 予定です (*yotei desu*) to talk about your intentions and future plans.

By the end of this chapter, you'll be able to confidently express your desires and plans, making your conversations more engaging and dynamic.

Let's start by understanding the **"Want to" Form**!

The "Want to" Form

In Japanese, expressing what you **want to do** is straightforward using the たい (*-tai*) form. This form is added to the **stem** of a verb and conjugates similarly to い-**adjectives**. Understanding how to use this form will allow you to express your desires clearly and naturally.

1. How to Form the たい (*-tai*) Structure

1. **Identify the verb's stem:**

    - For う-**Verbs**, change the last **-u** sound to its **-i** form (e.g., 書く → 書き - *kaku → kaki*).

    - For る-**Verbs**, simply drop る (e.g., 食べる → 食べ- *taberu → tabe*).

2. **Add たい to the stem:**

    - 書く (*kaku*) – To write → 書きたい (*kakitai*) – Want to write

    - 食べる (*taberu*) – To eat → 食べたい (*tabetai*) – Want to eat

Examples:

- 私は寿司を食べたいです。
  (*Watashi wa sushi o tabetai desu.*)
  Meaning: I want to eat sushi.

* 彼は本を書きたいです。
  (*Kare wa hon o kakitai desu.*)
  Meaning: He wants to write a book.

2. Negative Form: Want to Not Do

To express **not wanting to do** something, replace たい with たくない (*-takunai*).

Examples:

* 私は映画を見たくないです。
  (*Watashi wa eiga o mitakunai desu.*)
  Meaning: I don't want to watch a movie.
* 彼女は行きたくないです。
  (*Kanojo wa ikitakunai desu.*)
  Meaning: She doesn't want to go.

3. Past Tense of the "Want to" Form

The past tense is formed by changing たい to たかった (*-takatta*) for affirmative and たくなかった (*-takunakatta*) for negative.

Examples:

* 昨日ラーメンを食べたかったです。
  (*Kinou raamen o tabetakatta desu.*)
  Meaning: I wanted to eat ramen yesterday.
* 彼は来たくなかったです。
  (*Kare wa kitakunakatta desu.*)
  Meaning: He didn't want to come.

Using these forms, you can express your **wants** and **dislikes** for present and past situations.

Using the "I Plan to" and "I Intend to" Patterns

When you want to express your **intentions** or **plans** in Japanese, two common patterns are used: つもりです (*tsumori desu*) and 予定です (*yotei desu*). Each pattern conveys a different degree of certainty about your plans.

1. Using つもりです (*tsumori desu*) – "I Intend to"

* つもりです is used to express a **personal intention** or **will** to do something.
* It follows the **dictionary form** of the verb:

Verb	Structure	Meaning
行く (*iku*)	行くつもりです (*iku tsumori desu*)	I intend to go.
勉強する (*benkyou suru*)	勉強するつもりです (*benkyou suru tsumori desu*)	I intend to study.

Example Sentences:

- 私は明日、図書館に行くつもりです。
  (*Watashi wa ashita, toshokan ni iku tsumori desu.*)
  Meaning: I intend to go to the library tomorrow.
- 彼は大学で日本語を勉強するつもりです。
  (*Kare wa daigaku de nihongo o benkyou suru tsumori desu.*)
  Meaning: He intends to study Japanese at university.

Negative Form:

- つもりです → つもりはありません (*tsumori wa arimasen*)
- 行かないつもりです。(*Ikanai tsumori desu.*)
  Meaning: I do not intend to go.

2. Using 予定です (*yotei desu*) – "I Plan to"

- 予定です is used to express **plans** or **arrangements** that have a more concrete, scheduled aspect.
- It often includes **time expressions** and follows the **dictionary form** of the verb:

Verb	Structure	Meaning
会う (*au*)	会う予定です (*au yotei desu*)	I plan to meet.
出発する (*shuppatsu suru*)	出発する予定です (*shuppatsu suru yotei desu*)	I plan to depart.

Example Sentences:

- 来月、旅行する予定です。
  (*Raigetsu, ryokou suru yotei desu.*)
  Meaning: I plan to travel next month.

- 彼女は金曜日に友達と会う予定です。
  (*Kanojo wa kinyoubi ni tomodachi to au yotei desu.*)
  Meaning: She plans to meet her friend on Friday.

Negative Form:

- 予定です → 予定はありません (*yotei wa arimasen*)

- 来る予定はありません。(*Kuru yotei wa arimasen.*)
  Meaning: I have no plan to come.

3. Difference Between つもりです and 予定です

- **つもりです** (*tsumori desu*): Indicates a **personal intention**—what *you* are thinking of doing

- **予定です** (*yotei desu*): Indicates a **plan or schedule**—often involving external factors or commitments

Example:

- 私は来週日本に行くつもりです。
  (*Watashi wa raishuu Nihon ni iku tsumori desu.*)
  Meaning: I intend to go to Japan next week.
  (Personal intention)

- 私は来週日本に行く予定です。
  (*Watashi wa raishuu Nihon ni iku yotei desu.*)
  Meaning: I have a plan to go to Japan next week.
  (Already scheduled plan)

Understanding this distinction will help you choose the appropriate pattern depending on the context.

Key Takeaways

- ❖ Use たい (*-tai*) to express what you want to do (e.g., 食べたい - want to eat). For the negative form, use たくない (*-takunai*), and for past tense, use たかった (*-takatta*).

- ❖ つもりです (*tsumori desu*): Used to express **personal intentions** (e.g., 行くつもりです - I intend to go.)

- ❖ 予定です (*yotei desu*): Used for **scheduled plans** (e.g., 旅行する予定です - I plan to travel.)

- ❖ つもりはありません and 予定はありません: Used to express **lack of intention or plan** (e.g., 来る予定はありません - I have no plan to come.)

Exercises

Exercise 1: Sentence Completion

Complete the sentences using the correct **たい** form:

1. 私は日本語を＿＿＿＿＿。(*watashi wa nihongo o ＿＿＿＿＿.*)
   Meaning: I want to study Japanese.
     - Options: 勉強したい, 勉強します, 勉強する

2. 彼女はパスタを＿＿＿＿＿。(*kanojo wa pasuta o ＿＿＿＿＿.*)
   Meaning: She wants to eat pasta.
     - Options: 食べたい, 食べます, 食べる

3. 子供たちは公園で＿＿＿＿＿。(*kodomotachi wa kouen de ＿＿＿＿＿.*)
   Meaning: The children want to play at the park.
     - Options: 遊びたい, 遊びます, 遊ぶ

Exercise 2: Choosing the Correct Form

Select the appropriate form to express **intention** or **plan**:

1. 私は今日家で映画を見＿＿＿＿＿。(*watashi wa kyou ie de eiga o mi ＿＿＿＿＿.*)
   Meaning: I intend to watch a movie at home today.
     - Options: つもりです, 予定です, たいです

2. 彼は来週京都に行く＿＿＿＿＿。(*kare wa raishuu Kyoto ni iku ＿＿＿＿＿.*)
   Meaning: He has a plan to go to Kyoto next week.
     - Options: たいです, 予定です, つもりです

3. 明日友達と会う＿＿＿＿＿。(*ashita tomodachi to au ＿＿＿＿＿.*)
   Meaning: I plan to meet my friend tomorrow.
     - Options: 予定です, つもりです, たいです

Exercise 3: Translation Practice

Translate the following sentences into Japanese using the appropriate patterns:

1. I want to go to Japan.
2. She does not intend to come.
3. I plan to study English next year.
4. He wanted to eat ramen yesterday.
5. We plan to travel next month.

Answer Key

Exercise 1: Sentence Completion

1. 私は日本語を**勉強したい**。
   (*Watashi wa nihongo o benkyou shitai.*)
   Meaning: I want to study Japanese.

2. 彼女はパスタを**食べたい**。
   (*Kanojo wa pasuta o tabetai.*)
   Meaning: She wants to eat pasta.

3. 子供たちは公園で**遊びたい**。
   (*Kodomotachi wa kouen de asobitai.*)
   Meaning: The children want to play at the park.

Exercise 2: Choosing the Correct Form

1. 私は今日家で映画を見**つもりです**。
   (*Watashi wa kyou ie de eiga o miru tsumori desu.*)
   Meaning: I intend to watch a movie at home today.

2. 彼は来週京都に行く**予定です**。
   (*Kare wa raishuu Kyoto ni iku yotei desu.*)
   Meaning: He has a plan to go to Kyoto next week.

3. 明日友達と会う**予定です**。
   (*Ashita tomodachi to au yotei desu.*)
   Meaning: I plan to meet my friend tomorrow.

Exercise 3: Translation Practice

1. I want to go to Japan.
   - 日本に行きたいです。
     (*Nihon ni ikitai desu.*)

2. She does not intend to come.
   - 彼女は来るつもりはありません。
     (*Kanojo wa kuru tsumori wa arimasen.*)

3. I plan to study English next year.
   - 来年、英語を勉強する予定です。
     (*Rainen, eigo o benkyou suru yotei desu.*)

4. He wanted to eat ramen yesterday.
   - 彼は昨日ラーメンを食べたかったです。
     (*Kare wa kinou raamen o tabetakatta desu.*)

5. We plan to travel next month.
   - 私たちは来月旅行する予定です。
     (*Watashitachi wa raigetsu ryokou suru yotei desu.*)

Chapter 6: Complex Sentence Patterns

"The art of communication is the language of leadership."
– James Humes

Being able to combine multiple ideas into a single, cohesive sentence is a significant step in advancing your Japanese skills. While simple sentences are effective for basic communication, expressing more nuanced thoughts often requires connecting ideas to form **compound** and **complex sentences**. This chapter will introduce you to the various ways to create more sophisticated sentence patterns using **conjunctions**, **relative clauses**, and **different verb forms**.

In this chapter, you'll learn how to:

1. **Combine Simple Sentences**: Use conjunctions to link two or more thoughts.
2. **Create Compound and Complex Sentences**: Understand how to connect sentences using **te-form**, **clauses**, and other grammar structures.

By the end, you'll be able to express more detailed ideas, describe events more accurately, and communicate your thoughts more fluently.

Let's start by learning how to **combine simple sentences** to form more complex thoughts!

Combining Simple Sentences

Combining simple sentences in Japanese often involves using **conjunctions** or the **te-form** of verbs. This allows you to express multiple ideas smoothly without repeating subjects or verbs.

1. Using Conjunctions to Link Ideas

Conjunctions like **そして** (*soshite* - and), **しかし** (*shikashi* - but), and **だから** (*dakara* - therefore) are used to connect separate sentences.

Examples:

- 私は学生です。**そして、**アルバイトをしています。
  (*Watashi wa gakusei desu. Soshite, arubaito o shiteimasu.*)
  Meaning: I am a student. And, I have a part-time job.
- 映画を見た。**しかし、**面白くなかった。
  (*Eiga o mita. Shikashi, omoshirokunakatta.*)
  Meaning: I watched a movie. However, it wasn't interesting.

2. Using the Te-Form to Connect Actions

The **te-form** of verbs is commonly used to show a sequence of actions or describe related activities.

Verb	Te-Form	Meaning
食べる (*taberu*)	食べて (*tabete*)	To eat → Eating
行く (*iku*)	行って (*itte*)	To go → Going
書く (*kaku*)	書いて (*kaite*)	To write → Writing

Examples:

- ご飯を食べて、学校に行きます。
  (*Gohan o tabete, gakkou ni ikimasu.*)
  Meaning: I eat breakfast and go to school.
- 本を読んで、寝ました。
  (*Hon o yonde, nemashita.*)
  Meaning: I read a book and then slept.

The **te-form** acts like a **connector**, allowing you to combine multiple actions into a single sentence.

Creating Compound and Complex Sentences

The Japanese language uses **clauses**, **relative pronouns**, and **varied verb forms** to express more intricate ideas to create compound and complex sentences. These structures help convey cause-effect relationships, contrasts, and conditions.

1. Using から (*kara*) and ので (*node*) – "Because"

- から (*kara*) and ので (*node*) both mean "because," but ので is slightly more formal.

  Examples:

  - 私は疲れたから、早く寝ます。
    (*Watashi wa tsukareta kara, hayaku nemasu.*)
    Meaning: I'm tired, so I'll go to bed early.
  - 雨が降ったので、試合は中止です。
    (*Ame ga futta node, shiai wa chuushi desu.*)
    Meaning: Because it rained, the game is canceled.

**2. Using が (*ga*) and けど (*kedo*) – "But"

- が (*ga*) and けど (*kedo*) both mean "but" and connect contrasting ideas.

Examples:

- この本は面白い**けど**、高いです。
  (*Kono hon wa omoshiroi kedo, takai desu.*)
  Meaning: This book is interesting, but it's expensive.
- 行きたい**が**、時間がありません。
  (*Ikitai ga, jikan ga arimasen.*)
  Meaning: I want to go, but I don't have time.

3. Relative Clauses with "That" or "Which"
In Japanese, **relative clauses** come **before** the noun they describe:

Example:

- 私が昨日買った本。
  (*Watashi ga kinou katta hon.*)
  Meaning: The book **that I bought yesterday**.

Mastering these structures allows you to connect ideas fluidly and express complex relationships in a single sentence.

Key Takeaways

- ❖ Use **conjunctions** like **そして** (*soshite* - and), **しかし** (*shikashi* - but), and **だから** (*dakara* - therefore) to link simple sentences.
- ❖ The **te-form** is used to connect actions and indicate a sequence (e.g., 食べる → 食べて - eat → eating).
- ❖ **から** (*kara*) and **ので** (*node*) express **because**, while **が** (*ga*) and **けど** (*kedo*) indicate **but**.
- ❖ Relative clauses come **before** the noun they describe (e.g., *私が作った料理* - The dish **I made**).

Exercises

Exercise 1: Sentence Completion

Complete the sentences using the appropriate conjunction or form:

1. 昨日、映画を見ました。＿＿＿＿＿、面白かったです。 (*Kinou, eiga o mimashita. ＿＿＿＿＿, omoshirokatta desu.*)
   - Options: だから, しかし, そして
     Meaning: Yesterday, I watched a movie. ＿＿＿＿＿, it was interesting.

2. 私は疲れた＿＿＿＿＿、休みます。 (*Watashi wa tsukareta ＿＿＿＿＿, yasumimasu.*)
   - Options: から, けど, ので
     Meaning: I'm tired, so I'll rest.

3. ご飯を食べて、＿＿＿＿＿。 (*Gohan o tabete, ＿＿＿＿＿.*)
   - Options: 勉強しました, 行きます, 来ます
     Meaning: I ate dinner and ＿＿＿＿＿.

Exercise 2: Relative Clauses

Create a single sentence using relative clauses:

1. **I bought a book. / It is expensive.**
   Hint: The book **that I bought** is expensive.

2. **He met a friend. / The friend lives in Tokyo.**
   Hint: The friend **whom he met** lives in Tokyo.

Exercise 3: Translation Practice

Translate the following sentences into Japanese using the appropriate complex sentence patterns:

1. I want to go, but I have no money.
2. I will go to the park and take a walk.
3. Because it's raining, I will stay home.
4. The movie I watched yesterday was boring.
5. I plan to study, but I don't have time.

Answer Key

Exercise 1: Sentence Completion

1. 昨日、映画を見ました。**そして**、面白かったです。
   (*Kinou, eiga o mimashita. Soshite, omoshirokatta desu.*)
   Meaning: Yesterday, I watched a movie. And, it was interesting.

2. 私は疲れた**から**、休みます。
   (*Watashi wa tsukareta kara, yasumimasu.*)
   Meaning: I'm tired, so I'll rest.

3. ご飯を食べて、**勉強しました**。
   (*Gohan o tabete, benkyou shimashita.*)
   Meaning: I ate dinner and studied.

Exercise 2: Relative Clauses

1. **I bought a book. / It is expensive.**

   - 私が買った本は高いです。
     (*Watashi ga katta hon wa takai desu.*)
     Meaning: The book that I bought is expensive.

2. **He met a friend. / The friend lives in Tokyo.**

   - 彼が会った友達は東京に住んでいます。
     (*Kare ga atta tomodachi wa Toukyou ni sundeimasu.*)
     Meaning: The friend whom he met lives in Tokyo.

Exercise 3: Translation Practice

1. I want to go, but I have no money.

   - 行きたいですが、お金がありません。
     (*Ikitai desu ga, okane ga arimasen.*)

2. I will go to the park and take a walk.

   - 公園に行って、散歩します。
     (*Kouen ni itte, sanpo shimasu.*)

3. Because it's raining, I will stay home.

   - 雨が降っているので、家にいます。
     (*Ame ga futteiru node, ie ni imasu.*)

4. The movie I watched yesterday was boring.

   - 私が昨日見た映画はつまらなかったです。
     (*Watashi ga kinou mita eiga wa tsumaranakatta desu.*)

5. I plan to study, but I don't have time.

   - 勉強する予定ですが、時間がありません。
     (*Benkyou suru yotei desu ga, jikan ga arimasen.*)

Chapter 7: Using Particles Effectively

"Particles are the glue that holds Japanese sentences together."
– Unknown

Particles are small but powerful words that define the **function** of other words in a sentence, such as marking the **subject, object, location,** or **direction**. Mastering particles is crucial because they clarify **who** is doing **what, where,** and **how** in any given statement.

This chapter will provide a comprehensive overview of the **core particles** in Japanese and their essential roles, including:

1. は (*wa*) – Topic marker
2. が (*ga*) – Subject marker
3. を (*wo*) – Direct object marker
4. に (*ni*) – Direction, time, or purpose marker
5. で (*de*) – Location or means marker

By understanding and using these particles correctly, you'll be able to construct clear, nuanced sentences and express yourself more accurately.

Let's dive into the **overview of key particles** to see how each one functions!

Overview of Key Particles: は, が, を, に, で

Particles indicate the **grammatical role** of words in a sentence, helping to define **subjects, objects, locations,** and more. Here's an overview of the essential particles you need to master:

1. は (*wa*) – Topic Marker

- Marks the **topic** of the sentence, indicating what the statement is about
- Often translated as "as for" or "speaking of"

   Example:

   - 私は学生です。 (*Watashi wa gakusei desu.*)
     Meaning: I am a student.
     (*Topic: 私 / I*)

2. が (*ga*) – Subject Marker

- Highlights the **subject** that performs the action
- Used when introducing **new information** or **emphasizing** the subject

Example:

- 猫がいます。 (*Neko ga imasu.*)
  Meaning: There is a cat.
  (Subject: 猫 / Cat)

3. を (*wo*) – Direct Object Marker

- Marks the **direct object** of an action, showing what is being acted upon

  Example:

  - 本を読みます。 (*Hon o yomimasu.*)
    Meaning: I read a book.
    (Object: 本 / Book)

4. に (*ni*) – Direction, Time, or Purpose Marker

- Indicates the **direction** of an action, **specific time**, or **purpose**.

  Examples:

  - 学校に行きます。 (*Gakkou ni ikimasu.*)
    Meaning: I go to school.
    (Direction: 学校 / School)

  - 7時に起きます。 (*Shichi-ji ni okimasu.*)
    Meaning: I wake up at 7 o'clock.
    (Time: 7時 / 7 o'clock)

  - 友達に会います。 (*Tomodachi ni aimasu.*)
    Meaning: I meet my friend.
    (Purpose: 友達 / Friend)

5. で (*de*) – Location or Means Marker

- Indicates the **location** of an action or the **means** by which an action is performed

  Examples:

  - 図書館で勉強します。 (*Toshokan de benkyou shimasu.*)
    Meaning: I study at the library.
    (Location: 図書館 / Library)

  - バスで行きます。 (*Basu de ikimasu.*)
    Meaning: I go by bus.
    (Means: バス / Bus)

Sentence Examples and Practice

Let's see how these particles function in context. Here are some sample sentences:

1. は (*wa*) vs. が (*ga*)

- は introduces the **topic**, while が emphasizes the **subject**.

  Examples:

  - 私は日本語が好きです。
    (*Watashi wa Nihongo ga suki desu.*)
    Meaning: I like Japanese.
    (*Topic: 私 / I, Subject: 日本語 / Japanese*)
  - 犬は猫が嫌いです。
    (*Inu wa neko ga kirai desu.*)
    Meaning: The dog dislikes cats.
    (*Topic: 犬 / Dog, Subject: 猫 / Cats*)

2. を (*wo*) – Direct Object Marker

  Examples:

  - 映画を見ます。
    (*Eiga o mimasu.*)
    Meaning: I watch a movie.
    (*Object: 映画 / Movie*)

3. に (*ni*) – Direction, Time, or Purpose

  Examples:

  - 午後6時に帰ります。
    (*Gogo roku-ji ni kaerimasu.*)
    Meaning: I return at 6 p.m.
    (*Time: 午後6時 / 6 p.m.*)
  - 公園に行きます。
    (*Kouen ni ikimasu.*)
    Meaning: I go to the park.
    (*Direction: 公園 / Park*)

4. で (*de*) – Location or Means

  Examples:

  - 車で来ます。
    (*Kuruma de kimasu.*)

Meaning: I come by car.
(Means: 車 / Car)

- レストランで食べます。
  (Resutoran de tabemasu.)
  Meaning: I eat at the restaurant.
  (Location: レストラン / Restaurant)

Key Takeaways

❖ **は (*wa*)**: Marks the **topic** of the sentence, indicating what the statement is about

❖ **が (*ga*)**: Highlights the **subject**, often used to introduce new information or emphasize a point

❖ **を (*wo*)**: Marks the **direct object** of an action

❖ **に (*ni*)**: Indicates **direction**, **time**, or **purpose**

❖ **で (*de*)**: Shows the **location** of an action or the **means** by which an action is carried out

Exercises

Exercise 1: Fill in the Missing Particles

Complete the sentences below with the correct particle:

1. 私＿＿＿＿＿日本語を勉強します。(*Watashi ＿＿＿＿＿ Nihongo o benkyou shimasu.*)
   Meaning: I study Japanese.
   - Options: は, が, に

2. 彼は明日学校＿＿＿＿＿行きます。(*Kare wa ashita gakkou ＿＿＿＿＿ ikimasu.*)
   Meaning: He will go to school tomorrow.
   - Options: で, を, に

3. レストラン＿＿＿＿＿食べます。(*Resutoran ＿＿＿＿＿ tabemasu.*)
   Meaning: I eat at the restaurant.
   - Options: で, に, は

4. 図書館＿＿＿＿＿本を読みます。(*Toshokan ＿＿＿＿＿ hon o yomimasu.*)
   Meaning: I read books at the library.
   - Options: を, で, に

5. 私は午後5時＿＿＿＿＿帰ります。(*Watashi wa gogo go-ji ＿＿＿＿＿ kaerimasu.*)
   Meaning: I return at 5 p.m.
   - Options: に, が, を

Exercise 2: Sentence Translation

Translate the following sentences into Japanese using the correct particles:

1. I go to the park by bicycle.
2. He meets his friend at 2 p.m.
3. I eat sushi at the restaurant.
4. There is a cat in the garden.
5. She reads a book at school.

Answer Key

Exercise 1: Fill in the Missing Particles

1. 私**は**日本語**を**勉強します。
   (*Watashi wa Nihongo o benkyou shimasu.*)
   Meaning: I study Japanese.

2. 彼**は**明日学校**に**行きます。
   (*Kare wa ashita gakkou ni ikimasu.*)
   Meaning: He will go to school tomorrow.

3. レストラン**で**食べます。
   (*Resutoran de tabemasu.*)
   Meaning: I eat at the restaurant.

4. 図書館**で**本**を**読みます。
   (*Toshokan de hon o yomimasu.*)
   Meaning: I read books at the library.

5. 私**は**午後5時**に**帰ります。
   (*Watashi wa gogo go-ji ni kaerimasu.*)
   Meaning: I return at 5 p.m.

Exercise 2: Sentence Translation

1. I go to the park by bicycle.
   - 自転車**で**公園**に**行きます。
     (*Jitensha de kouen ni ikimasu.*)

2. He meets his friend at 2 p.m.
   - 彼**は**午後2時**に**友達**に**会います。
     (*Kare wa gogo ni-ji ni tomodachi ni aimasu.*)

3. I eat sushi at the restaurant.
   - レストラン**で**寿司**を**食べます。
     (*Resutoran de sushi o tabemasu.*)

4. There is a cat in the garden.
   - 庭**に**猫**が**います。
     (*Niwa ni neko ga imasu.*)

5. She reads a book at school.
   - 彼女**は**学校**で**本**を**読みます。
     (*Kanojo wa gakkou de hon o yomimasu.*)

Chapter 8: Question Forms and Politeness Levels

"Politeness is not just a matter of language—it's a reflection of culture."
– Unknown

In Japanese, asking questions and making requests can vary greatly depending on the level of **politeness** required. Japanese offers a wide range of forms to express politeness, from casual speech with friends to highly formal language used in business settings. Understanding how to adjust your speech according to context is essential for effective communication.

In this chapter, you'll learn:

1. How to **form questions** and **make requests** in both casual and formal settings
2. How to use **politeness markers** and understand when to switch between **casual** and **formal** speech
3. Key differences between **neutral** (です／ます), **casual**, and **honorific** language

By the end, you'll be able to navigate different social situations comfortably, ask questions, and make requests with the appropriate level of politeness.

Let's start by learning the basics of **making questions and requests**!

Making Questions and Requests

1. Making Questions

In Japanese, turning a statement into a question is simple: add the particle **か** (*ka*) at the end of the sentence.

Examples:

- これは何ですか？
  (*Kore wa nan desu ka?*)
  Meaning: What is this?

- あなたは学生ですか？
  (*Anata wa gakusei desu ka?*)
  Meaning: Are you a student?

For **casual questions**, simply raise your intonation without adding **か**:

Example:

- どこに行くの？
  (*Doko ni iku no?*)
  Meaning: Where are you going?

2. Making Requests

Requests are made using **verb conjugations** or special request forms:

- ~てください (*~te kudasai*): Used for polite requests
  Example:
  - 窓を閉めてください。
    (*Mado o shimete kudasai.*)
    Meaning: Please close the window.
- ~てくれる？ (*~te kureru?*): Casual request form
  Example:
  - ドアを開けてくれる？
    (*Doa o akete kureru?*)
    Meaning: Can you open the door?
- ~てもらえますか？ (*~te moraemasu ka?*): Politer form for asking for help
  Example:
  - これを見てもらえますか？
    (*Kore o mite moraemasu ka?*)
    Meaning: Could you take a look at this?

Casual vs. Formal Speech

Japanese has three primary speech levels: **casual**, **polite**, and **formal**. The level you choose depends on **who** you're speaking to and **the context**.

1. Casual Speech

- Used with **friends**, **family**, or **people of the same age/status**
- Typically drops です/ます endings

  Examples:
  - 行く？ (*Iku?*) – Going?
  - 見るよ。 (*Miru yo.*) – I'll watch it.

2. Polite Speech

- Used in **neutral** settings, such as speaking to **strangers**, **colleagues**, or in **general conversations**
- Uses です/ます endings

  Examples:
  - 行きますか？ (*Ikimasu ka?*) – Will you go?
  - 見ます。 (*Mimasu.*) – I will watch.

3. Formal Speech / Honorific Language (敬語: *keigo*)

- Used to show **respect** to **superiors**, **clients**, or in **business settings**
- Involves **complex verb conjugations** and honorific phrases

  Examples:

  - いらっしゃいますか？ (*Irasshaimasu ka?*) – Is [person] there?
  - 拝見します。 (*Haiken shimasu.*) – I will take a look.

Understanding which form to use ensures that your speech is **appropriate** and **respectful** in any situation.

Key Takeaways

- ❖ To **form questions**, add か (*ka*) at the end of a sentence (e.g., 行きますか - Will you go?).
- ❖ Use ~てください (*~te kudasai*) for polite requests, and ~てくれる？ (*~te kureru?*) for casual ones.
- ❖ Adjust your speech level based on the context:
  - ➢ **Casual**: Drops です／ます
  - ➢ **Polite**: Uses です／ます endings
  - ➢ **Formal/Honorific**: Uses specialized forms to show respect (敬語 / *keigo*)

Exercises

Exercise 1: Sentence Completion

Complete the sentences using the appropriate question or request forms:

1. これは＿＿＿＿＿ですか？ (*Kore wa ＿＿＿＿＿ desu ka?*)
   Meaning: What is this?

   ○ Options: 何, 誰, どこ

2. ドアを＿＿＿＿＿ください。 (*Doa o ＿＿＿＿＿ kudasai.*)
   Meaning: Please open the door.

   ○ Options: 閉めて, 開けて, 消して

3. どこ＿＿＿＿＿行きますか？ (*Doko ＿＿＿＿＿ ikimasu ka?*)
   Meaning: Where are you going?

   ○ Options: に, が, で

4. これを見＿＿＿＿＿もらえますか？ (*Kore o mi＿＿＿＿＿ moraemasu ka?*)
   Meaning: Could you take a look at this?

   ○ Options: て, る, く

5. あなたは学生＿＿＿＿＿？ (*Anata wa gakusei ＿＿＿＿＿?*)
   Meaning: Are you a student?

   ○ Options: か, の, に

Exercise 2: Choose the Correct Speech Level

Choose the correct form for each context:

1. **Talking to a friend**:

   ○ 行く？ (*Iku?*) / 行きますか？ (*Ikimasu ka?*)

2. **Speaking with a teacher**:

   ○ 見る？ (*Miru?*) / ご覧になりますか？ (*Goran ni narimasu ka?*)

3. **Requesting help politely**:

   ○ 手伝ってくれる？ (*Tetsudatte kureru?*) / 手伝ってください (*Tetsudatte kudasai*)

4. **Asking a superior to check a document**:

   ○ これを見てください (*Kore o mite kudasai*) / 拝見していただけますか (*Haiken shite itadakemasu ka*)

5. **Talking to a stranger at a store**:

   ○ これ、いくら？ (*Kore, ikura?*) / これ、おいくらですか？ (*Kore, oikura desu ka?*)

Exercise 3: Translation Practice

Translate the following sentences into Japanese using the appropriate forms:

1. Can you help me?
2. What time is it?
3. Please close the window.
4. Are you coming tomorrow?
5. Where is the restroom?

Answer Key

Exercise 1: Sentence Completion

1. これは何ですか？
   (*Kore wa nan desu ka?*)
   Meaning: What is this?

2. ドアを開けてください。
   (*Doa o akete kudasai.*)
   Meaning: Please open the door.

3. どこに行きますか？
   (*Doko ni ikimasu ka?*)
   Meaning: Where are you going?

4. これを見てもらえますか？
   (*Kore o mite moraemasu ka?*)
   Meaning: Could you take a look at this?

5. あなたは学生ですか？
   (*Anata wa gakusei desu ka?*)
   Meaning: Are you a student?

Exercise 2: Choose the Correct Speech Level

1. **Talking to a friend**:
   - 行く？ (*Iku?*)
     (*Casual form for friends.*)

2. **Speaking with a teacher**:
   - ご覧になりますか？ (*Goran ni narimasu ka?*)
     (*Honorific form for superiors.*)

3. **Requesting help politely**:
   - 手伝ってください (*Tetsudatte kudasai*)
     (*Polite request form.*)

4. **Asking a superior to check a document**:
   - 拝見していただけますか (*Haiken shite itadakemasu ka*)
     (*Honorific form for checking a document.*)

5. **Talking to a stranger at a store**:
   - これ、おいくらですか？ (*Kore, oikura desu ka?*)
     (*Polite question for unknown people.*)

1. Can you help me?
   ○ 手伝ってくれますか？
   (*Tetsudatte kuremasu ka?*)
2. What time is it?
   ○ 何時ですか？
   (*Nan-ji desu ka?*)
3. Please close the window.
   ○ 窓を閉めてください。
   (*Mado o shimete kudasai.*)
4. Are you coming tomorrow?
   ○ 明日来ますか？
   (*Ashita kimasu ka?*)
5. Where is the restroom?
   ○ トイレはどこですか？
   (*Toire wa doko desu ka?*)

Conclusion

Great job! You've mastered key grammar, vocabulary, and sentence structures needed for effective communication in Japanese. From forming questions to using the right level of politeness, you now have a solid foundation.

Remember, language learning is a journey. Keep practicing, expanding your vocabulary, and applying what you've learned in real conversations.

Keep going—がんばってください (*Ganbatte kudasai* - Keep up the good work)!

Let us know if you'd like to continue or have any questions!